Contents

Section Two: Writing Poems

Chapter Three: *Generate a Poem*   22

Chapter Four: *Advanced Exercises*   36

Introduction

Why write poetry? Certainly, there are as many answers to this question as there are people to give such answers voice. We have often described poetry to our students as a space, somewhere one can go to experience things that are not easily found elsewhere in our lives. Poetry is room we can walk into with absolute honesty, for example, or in the guise of a person other than ourselves. Because it is creative space, artistic space, we have more freedom there—but also some responsibility. Writing poetry responsibly means taking the task seriously enough to want to educate oneself about the ways in which it has been and is being done. (Thus, all serious writers of contemporary poetry make it their mission to read poems every day and to study how poems have been and are being made.) To create art, however, one must also be prepared to break rules, to step outside forms and expectations to find ways of writing and speaking that surprise perhaps even ourselves. This is the paradox of poetry writing: to revere the past and the present, yet keep an eye on the freedom to explore so that we may have the opportunity to do something innovative in the future. Poetry is a remarkable space. . . and the rewards of entering it are equally many.

For creative writing classes, writing groups, or individual writers, we believe in "inspiration" but not in waiting for it. Why? First, because none of us—and particularly student writers—can count on inspiration blossoming within timetables neatly accommodating any deadlines we might be under. The other reason is that when artists gather in a studio, the goal is not necessarily to produce great works of art but to produce "studies." Our goal is to foster first better poets in the long run, and second better poems during the course of a semester or during any period of writing activity. Just as practice sessions for sports teams prepare athletes for "the big game," as writers, we must be limber and flexible, in shape and ready for the moment when we get that touch of inspiration on the shoulder. The practices presented in *Double Bloom* prepare the way for any good poems that follow, for often a writer is found by a subject (rather than the other way around) and ignites it with the power of language.

The sampling of student poems appended to *Double Bloom's* exercises is intended to be an instructive selection of examples. They illustrate many of the possibilities the exercises invite. Our guiding principles in choosing them were (1) Do we like the poem? (2) Does it seem to reflect the essence of the exercise? and (3) Are its craft and artistic features discernible to the average reader and of interest? If the answer is clearly "yes" to all three, it is presented here. This book is written out of these practices and strategies—and from the remarkable communities of learning that have bloomed under them. We are grateful to our students at Corning Community College, Ohio University and Ohio University—Lancaster, Bowling Green State University, Elmira College, and elsewhere for the opportunity to work with you.

Finally, a note about the title. We call this book "Double Bloom" because writing poetry—creating the ideas and language that constitute it—is often a surprising experience, much like a "double bloom" in the world of horticulture, where two flowers blossom on a single stem of camellias, marguerites or begonias, for example. This surprise, interestingly enough, is also often mirrored in poetry writing "exercises." Creative activities are more mysterious than we may imagine.

Preface

This book of poetry writing exercises is designed to stimulate the creative imagination by creating the circumstances, or at least one set of them, under which poems come to life. Its instructional design assumes that actively practicing poetry writing under the right stimuli is a strong addition to any poet's development and is, in itself, a powerful learning tool in artistic exploration and creative work. These exercises are part of an active-learning strategy that assumes that most of us have valuable things to say if we can just seek them out and frame the search in meaningful or interesting ways.

Double Bloom is composed of five individual chapters organized into two generalized sections. Section One includes Chapter One: *Reading, Listening, and Responding* and Chapter Two: *Group Exercises*. Chapters Three, Four and Five are titled *Generate a Poem, Advanced Exercises* and *Revision,* respectively, and included in Section Two. The first section is designed as an introduction to some of the techniques that people who love to teach poetry use as a matter of course, including a number of group writing exercises appropriate for the college classroom or a writer's group. First, in Chapter One, we introduce readers to The Writer's Notebook and suggest a few ways to fill it (though there is certainly no limit to how each of us might do so!) Other exercises in this chapter, such as Spinning Cliches into Gold, recognize what all careful readers know about language and phrasing: it must be unusual or unexpected in order to be striking. The Poem Purchase and Construct an Anthology, on the other hand, ask us to familiarize ourselves with our own likes and dislikes, in part by creating a personal "collection" of poems published by others through which we can hunt for our own aesthetic sensibilities. In this chapter, we also provide an opportunity to "kill" a good poem by making concrete words abstract and specific words more general in nature. All of the exercises in Chapter One are designed to help us analyze our own responses to poetry and sharpen the tools of language that are needed to write good poems.

Next, Chapter Two is composed of activities that may be done with others, though many of these exercises are fully adaptable for individuals writing on their own as well. Writing collaboratively is a good way to begin utilizing some of the tools recognized and developed in the first chapter. But perhaps its most significant feature is the gift of collaboration itself. The panoramic view of the imagination that is possible when we encounter a poem written by twenty people is often remarkable and instructive. The great variety of our individual imaginations is on display in such an exercise, and one interesting imaginative idea often generates another. In fact, most writers rely on it: this is why all good writers often read a little (or a lot) before they write a single word. Finally, there is also something magical in sharing our creative impulses; it builds community in interesting ways, and all artists benefit from community. This is why writer's workshops developed in the first place, out of some sense of the remarkable benefits generated by artistic communities in places like Paris, London, or New York—although these days, with the right group of people, any good coffee shop will do.

Section Two—which includes Chapters Three, Four and Five—is the heart of this book, literally and figuratively. In Chapters Three and Four of this section, we present forty-two exercises that generate an original poem. Many of these come with variations; thus the number of poems generated by working out of these two sections is even higher. And, of course, one can always choose to write more than one version or draft of any single exercise. In fact, when we teach out of this book we always urge our students to find the exercises they like best and use them often to create multiple drafts. We ask students to try each exercise in Chapters Three and Four at least once and then focus on the ones they enjoy in order to make further use more fruitful. We also urge students never to give up completely on an exercise, even if they do not enjoy it the first time through. The more we write, the more our perspectives with regard to poetry writing change. The exercise that doesn't strike us right away may be a gold mine in six months or a year from now.

Some of the exercises in Chapters Three and Four ask writers to place themselves in interesting scenarios as a way of stimulating the imagination. Others ask writers to take their notebooks and physically relocate in order to take advantage of certain physical spaces, the moods that they evoke or the opportunities they provide simply to listen and hear. Still others suggest that writers draw on the page (as a method of providing thoughtful "pacing" through an idea or set of emotions), do a little research about the natural world, write a draft in traditional forms adapted for contemporary practitioners, pretend to be someone else, imitate the tone of a translation, write in a conversational style, draft a surrealistic poem, and more. These exercises are deliberately varied in nature because they are an attempt to reflect the complexity of the creative imagination and impulse as well as the intricate nature of the creative process, which always seeks something new, something innovative or striking.

Finally, Chapter Five: Revision—and, because we believe firmly that new forms create "new poems," the last exercise in Chapter Four—present techniques for revisiting a completed draft of a poem. Revision is the heart of poetry writing and all good writing, generally speaking. Much has been written about its value. The trick is to re-imagine the draft "critically" and then respond with potential changes, seeking always to imagine how it may be transformed in order to make it better, deeper, richer. Sometimes this means taking words away, and sometimes it indicates adding them. There are also occasions where entire drafts need to be set aside and the poem re-imagined from the start; or the forms of poems, line and stanza breaks, need to be reset and reconfigured, either lightly or radically. We always urge students and practicing writers to keep all of their drafts. We never know when we might want to retrace our steps and grab the tow rope we began with. Also, it is more liberating in terms of attempting revision techniques when we know that we already have a completed draft that is safe in its file (virtual or literal). In Chapter Five, we practice careful editing both to remove and add text to a draft, reworking the shape of lines in a poem, and generating multiple spin-offs of an original draft (as a way of seeing if we've captured the whole picture of the poem's subject). Chapter Five even offers some advice with regard to how whole books of poems are written. (This valuable piece of insight comes to us from Professor David Citino of The Ohio State University via Philip Terman of Clarion University.)

Section One: Warm Up

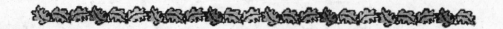

Chapter One

Reading, Listening, Responding

❧

❧ The Writer's Notebook

The Exercise

Find a blank notebook, preferably one with a sewn binding—not spiral bound—so you can't tear anything out. Some writers use the cheapest possible copybooks, so they feel free to write any old junk that comes to mind, especially while doing the exercises, while others like more pricey books. The key, though, is to select something that you want to use often, are not afraid to carry with you or be seen with, and is easy to pick up and jot things in.

Decorate it in any way that inspires you to write.

Be sure to date each entry. Some writers also put the time and place for each as well to really locate that entry in the context of their lives.

Now, fill it!

The Purpose

The Writer's Notebook is a place to build your powers of observation, to mine your memory, to expand and exercise your imagination, and to play with language. It is not a diary where you recount the day's events or process your emotional responses. In short, it is how you practice the skills and habits of being a writer. If poems come, great; if not, keep practicing. As the poet Theodore Roethke wrote in his notebook, "Make ready for your gifts. Prepare. Prepare."

❧ Spinning Clichés into Gold

The Exercise
Brainstorm a list of common clichés. "White as…," "Black as…," "Face turned (color for fear) as a…," "Face turned (color for anger) as a…," "It was cold as…," "Eyes as blue as…" et cetera. Try to generate a list of five to eight examples.

Clichés are simply attempts to make the abstract more concrete, so return to the experience itself and more fully imagine it, then take the image in a new direction. In other words, turn the cliché into a line that no one has ever heard before; strive for originality. Try for several for each one, allowing for weirdness, humor, or pain.

The Purpose
"Spinning Clichés…" helps make us aware of phrases that are too tired to use "as is," and gives us practice in creating comparisons and developing more original images. This exercise can also highlight when metaphors go too far and become funny (unintentionally), an important border to keep an eye on. (On the other hand, Foghorn Leghorn, the Warner Brothers' cartoon character, is famous for his original wise-cracking analogies like, "That boy's about as sharp as a bowling ball!" Although this simile is simplistic, it has so much home-spun color that we love it. The effect of a good original simile can be long-lasting.)

❧ An Image Album

The Exercise
In your Writer's Notebook, describe images from your day—like snapshots gathered in a photo album. This is descriptive writing, so avoid telling the "story" of what happened. See if you can catch people at a moment when their physical appearance expresses their personality or emotion, but write only what you see, like taking a picture. Try writing still life paintings of objects you saw that remain with you; create different angles perhaps of one object/scene or look for a variety of subjects to create different moods. It's important to see this as practice, so don't wait until images grab you or you feel "inspired" to do this! Do it now; do it often.

Variation I: Using items from your Memory Storehouse, write images of photographs that were never taken in your past.

Variation II: Take your notebook with you, and like an artist's sketchbook, write images you observe in the moment during the day, still striving for the instant that reveals through what is visible.

The Purpose
Writing images heightens our attention to our daily experience and practices observing closely to select details of greatest meaning. These powerful specifics in poems can go beyond the image to embody symbolic value as well. In the meantime, such writing also builds a habit of writing.

❧ The Memory Storehouse

The Exercise

Create a chart to list people, places, events, objects, and impressions from your memory. Add to it whenever they strike you, but remain open to the memories and encourage as many to rise to the surface of consciousness as possible.

As you do this, the lists may not be orderly: you may remember places as you recall people, so especially at first jot it all down and worry about the categories later. If what you remember is important, you can sort and organize after you recollect. You might think of memories as events that happened, so list them as they come to you, but these prompts will try to open the storehouse through other doors.

Consider the many people you've encountered. Picture elementary school—list teachers, students, coaches, and others—then move on to high school or college. Recall the outsiders and those passing through. Imagine church or temple—list leaders, worshippers, and folks at "the fringe." Think about your neighborhood—list kids, parents, people who moved away. Remember camp or vacations. Recall your family—immediate to extended and then friends of relatives. Think of people you associate with feelings—list people who let you down, who aroused you, who angered you, who delighted you, who embarrassed you, who loved you…don't forget those people *you* let down or frightened or thrilled or…. Consider folks linked to important lessons— those who taught you respect, the meaning of friendship, or how to do something that when you do it you think of even now.

Now, think of places: list houses you lived in, stores, places you worked, secret hideouts, where you partied, the place you went to be safe, etc. Picture rooms—list the ones in schools or where you lived, in places you visited or wanted to get out of. Imagine odd places: list places where you walked or got scared, locations where you felt closest to God, places where history approached and touched you, spots you smile about just to recall.

Watch how, in the days following this exercise, your dreams may be visited from the past or other memories will bubble up: if so, jot them down too. Remember your Image Album too, and consider writing descriptions of memories.

As you do future exercises, you might refer to this Storehouse for inspiration.

The Purpose

Each of us has a wealth of experience stored in memory, so this exercise gathers it up so we can lay claim to it, own it, and (if we want) use it in poems or in our growth as persons. Later exercises draw on this enormous resource as well.

❧ A Harvest Basket

The Exercise
As you read, collect examples of passages that strike you and copy them into your Writer's Notebook. Be watchful for writing that startles you—because it precisely describes an experience that has remained ineffable until now—and for sentences that create clear and vivid images in you, for words that seem to sing. (In his own inimitable Zen style, our friend Wayne Dodd has described this as seeing something in writing that "I always thought, but didn't know.") It doesn't matter if these words appear in prose or in poetry, many sentences or merely phrases. Even news stories that captivate you can be copied into your Notebook.

Be sure to copy the title of the piece and the author, so if you want to use it later in your writing you can acknowledge it properly. Titles of articles, poems, essays, songs, and stories go inside quotation marks, while the names of books, CDs, magazines, and newspapers are italicized (or underlined).

The Purpose
Beginning a habit of copying others' writing gets us reading like writers, aware of the craft as well as the effect words can have. Collecting such examples can also be the springboard for our own writing as well; see The Cento, The Found Poem, Spin-offs, From the News, as possible exercises.

❧ The Poem Purchase
—by Beth Bentley

The Exercise
Gather a number of anthologies of contemporary poetry, ones addressing topics like nature, war, jazz, etc. and ones gathering generations of poets. Spread them around the room. Give yourself a fixed amount of time—about 45 minutes to an hour will be reasonable. Spend the whole period "grazing" in those books, shopping for the poem you like the best and the one you think is worst. When you find candidates, copy the title, poet and book, then keep looking. By the end of the time allotted, purchase the one you like best and one you dislike, and copy both *by hand*. Later, write a paragraph explaining what you like in the best poem and why you chose the worst one.

For the Writer's Notebook: Begin collecting lines from others' poems you like: truths that startle, images that surprise, ideas you disagree with, etc. by copying them into your Notebook. Be sure to write down the author's name and the title of the poem, too.

The Purpose
Can you imagine someone coming up in baseball who only knows Dizzy Dean, a guitar player who limits her knowledge to the blues of T-Bone Walker, or a student in architecture only being aware of the Gothic style of the Middle Ages? We find that many people who begin writing poetry have read poems mostly for school assignments, which often focuses on classic work. Students rarely choose and rarely are in touch with more recent work. This exercise provides a

good first step in that direction with regard to poetry; it also requires a little bit of time and a reasonable library of poetry anthologies.

The Poem Purchase allows us to experience a wide range of poetry in a short time. Our own preferences and tastes come to light, and at the same time we may (hopefully) build a respectful awareness of others likes and dislikes too. In copying a poem by hand, we often become more aware of its features and discover things we may have missed. This kind of attention to poetry can open deeper ways of reading.

❧ The Thing Itself (or Me, Myself, and I)

The Exercise
Using all your senses, pay attention to an object. Write a description of it as objectively as you can, as if you were performing a science experiment. Then adopt a mood, like affection, but not necessarily toward the object itself. Now describe the thing in such a way that your feeling comes through without ever saying how you feel or using synonyms for the mood.

Now try to begin describing in one mood and shift to a radically different feeling, say starting out in anger but moving into sadness, or ridicule into admiration. Again, avoid stating the feeling but maintain the mood in how you describe the thing itself. Use your lines to either reinforce those shifts or to smooth them out into a more unified whole.

The Purpose
This exercise focuses on the power of emotion to generate wordplay or phrasing that reflect the feeling through the selection of detail and connotations inherent in word choice rather than direct statement. The shifts in mood add to the intensity of the exercise and have the capability to generate unexpected ideas.

❧ Senses Wake Up!

The Exercise
Spend a few minutes sitting quietly with your eyes closed. Use your hearing to record sounds, your sense of touch for all tactile sensations, your smell for all fragrances and odors, and even your taste for all lingering sensations in your mouth. Then for a fixed period, free-write what you experienced—about fifteen minutes at first. Describe it in addition to naming it.

Put your pen down and spend a few moments just looking, then describe and name what you saw.

Variations: Some teachers have suggested focusing on one sense at a time, alternating between brief moments of concentration and free-writing. It's also effective to return to a piece and push yourself to describe sensations you initially only name. For example, instead of "the sound of a car passing" you might describe that sound as "a car's engine snored then sputtered once, twice, before revving evenly and fading out of range."

Another strongly recommended variation is to find similes and metaphors that seem to go with your specific descriptions. "The rain hitting the sill" might be expanded to "The rain hitting the sill like a hand" (simile) or "The rain's hand hit the sill" (metaphor) or "The rain hitting the hand of the sill" (metaphor).

The Purpose
In order to create a sensory experience that involves readers rather than one that just talks "at" them, we must turn our attention to the body and listen (not just hear), see (not just look at), and absorb (not just touch). Senses Wake Up! begins shifting attention to the details that our senses experience and grounds our language in those actualities rather than in our commentary on them or the conclusions we draw from them. It also helps us to become much more specific in our descriptions. As an added gift, such exercises help us to enjoy living in this moment, more fully aware.

❧ How Do You Mean "Cleave"?

The Exercise
Generate a list of as many words as you can think of that have a variety of meanings, like cleave (to cut apart and to cling to). Other examples include "lick" (lap with tongue, beat in a fight, salt for feeding deer or horses), "scratch," "run," "strike," "clean," "spring," and "base." Take a few and write out their meanings, perhaps with examples. Keep opening the meanings by thinking of the word in phrases ("to run around with" vs. "to run around on" or "runaway train" vs. "runaway teenager").

Then, use a dictionary to introduce unfamiliar uses, ones in specialized fields ("irons" in sailing is to be stuck).

Finally, open even further to other forms of the word, including other spellings that sound the same ("base" and "bass"). You can go even further to generate words with inexact (slant) rhymes and their meanings.

Variation: People have constructed poems that integrate many of these versatile words into them so that readers have to keep moving, the piece unfolding as the context reveals which meaning is intended at this particular moment in the poem, like in Stephen Dunn's "Corners."

Variation II: Try to create a poem that revolves around one word that holds many meanings (but is not literally *about* that word) while also working in some other multi-faceted words.

The Purpose
This exercise helps us to experience how even simple vocabulary conveys a range of meanings and uses that we recognize, especially in context. For some of these words, exploring their fullness helps us re-imagine the concrete experience that lies hidden in them. It also helps us to begin claiming for ourselves a wider range of that network of meanings.

❧ The Texture of Words I

The Exercise
Make a list of your favorite nouns—at least five but try to generate ten or more. Make a note of those that are concrete, specific things and put a star or asterisk next to them; for the general ones, put a "G" next to them. Then mark the ones that are abstract with an "A."

For each general noun, try to list more specific manifestations of that thing. An obvious example is "furniture: chair, couch, armoire…." See if one of your "specific" nouns can be made even more focused, like "chair: folding, wing-back, recliner…." Ask yourself, "What kind?" at each level to see if there's a more specific category below.

Next, take a few examples of abstract nouns and write specific actions or things that "illustrate" that idea. For example, "anger" could be "teeth clenched like a vise," or "an arsonist waving a gas can inside me."

The Purpose
This exercise helps to develop mental flexibility with words (by moving between categories of words and particulars). In addition, it also provides experience in translating abstractions into realized images.

❧ The Texture of Words II

The Exercise
Make a list of very common verbs, like *go*, *walk*, and *talk*. Again, come up with at least five but work toward ten or more. Then list adverbs (usually ending in "-ly"). The adverbs don't have to relate to the actions in the other list, but they can.

Now take a verb and a random adverb. Say you select *go* and *weakly*. Try to come up with a verb that roughly means the same thing. It's best if you can get one-word equivalents. Could "going weakly" be "slumping along"? "Acquiescing"? How about "coasting"? Try different adverbs with the same verb to generate more combinations. Then expand your choices and try other variations.

The Purpose
A writing teacher once told us, "When you see an adverb, kill it!" We didn't get the lesson until years later when we began to understand more deeply the value of precise word choice. This exercise helps us practice the idea that "precision in the use of nouns and verbs frees one from the muddiness of most modifiers," as Sam Hamill put it in "The Necessity to Speak."

❧ The Texture of Words III

The Exercise
Generate list of adjectives, maybe words you'd use to describe a man, then a list for a woman. Come up with 3-5 for physical features and 3-5 for personality. You might put down *slender*, *hairy*, and *pale* for physical and *talkative*, *mean*, and *loving* for personality.

Taking one word at a time, brainstorm all the words you can think of that mean the same thing. So *slender* might give you *thin, skinny, lean, petite, emaciated, bony, wiry, anorexic, waif-like, string-bean, lanky...*

For each list, try using the synonyms for the other gender. Do we say, "Bob's a petite guy," for example? Identify why we use some words in certain contexts; what's the feeling-meaning of each one?

The Purpose
While How Do You Mean "Cleave"? explored the multiple definitions or uses of individual words, this version of The Texture of Words shows that words which seem to mean similar things have connotations (or shades of meaning) that may actually distinguish them from one another. Choosing words for a writer is a sweet agony because these subtleties seem endless, making precision an elusive but worthy goal.

❧ Kill This Poem!
—adapted from John Balaban

The Exercise
Using a poem built on a strong, consistent image (like "Hay for the Horses," by Gary Snyder or "The Fish," by Mary Oliver), ruin it by making concrete words abstract (for example, "sigh" becomes "dejection") and specific words more general in nature (for example, "hay" becomes "vegetation"). Consider or discuss how your new version compares with the original.

The Purpose
This exercise helps us focus on and appreciate the effect precise words can create, particularly the way concrete, specific nouns and verbs can bring color to the word painting a poem tries to be. Ruining a poem this way can also reveal how specific language that appeals both to our senses and to our sense of linguistic sensuality conveys the image more deeply while also suggesting the feeling or idea in more precise and accurate ways.

❦ Constructing an Anthology

The Exercise
Make a habit of keeping copies of your favorite poems from your reading. If you photocopy them, be sure to get the writer's name and the book it's from. After you have collected eight or ten, ask yourself what criteria you seem to be using in making your selections. What do these poems have in common? How are they sometimes different? Is there a unifying principle at work or are your selections varied and random? Write a page trying to articulate these ideas and observations.

Go on collecting the best poems you can find. When you have at least twenty, read your anthology and write about the experience analyzing your selections and how they work or function as a group. Finally, ask someone else to read and react to your anthology. Compare their reactions to your own analysis.

Variation I: If you are in a class, begin gathering poems that achieve the lessons you're going over: the best images in poems, best use of connotation in word choice, most effective line breaks, best blend of sound devices and content, and most interesting use of line length. (The choice of techniques is bound only by your imagination.) Be sure to include a few poems that astonish you and make you say, "Oh my God, I wish I could write like that!"

Variation II: Gather 8-12 poems on a similar theme: peace, Biblical figures, memories from childhood, love, mourning, mythological characters, etc. Notice similarities, of course, but the differences should be clearer too. Write up your observations, like an introduction to help orient a reader to your anthology and allow him or her to pay attention more carefully.

The Purpose
This exercise in using and creating anthologies helps us read poetry more actively and makes us aware of our preferences, exploring our tastes as readers and understanding them. Finding models of the craft puts a standard before us as writers, encouraging us to hone our skill and not be satisfied too easily. Finally, reading more widely can help us identify images, metaphors, or even overall tones that poets can adopt when dealing with certain topics, ultimately helping us avoid clichés and overworked techniques.

❦

Chapter Two

Group Exercises

In our creative writing classes and writer's groups, we've found that group exercises produce results ranging from amusing to interesting to amazing. We maintain that poetic language and syntax are a bit of a mystery, so sometimes letting someone else finish our thoughts or responding to another's frees us from the constraint of our own intentions and widens our gaze to new terrain. It can produce surprises—startling phrases, delightful passages, effective techniques, or other results we may not have come upon if left to our own devices. Group exercises can be fun and interesting to try, but at their best and with a little reflection, they are also instructive.

In using group exercises, look for patterns, discoveries, oddness that borders on the profound. For example, a group poem can take on a narrative that is quite original (whereas our natural attachment to stories that are our own may actually limit us sometimes). If too many cooks can ruin a soup, the opposite is sometimes true in these group poems. The more minds that contribute, the stranger and more varied the collaboration. And strangeness in poetry is often a virtue because it reveals or creates energetic juxtapositions that come alive with possibilities— even if the possibility is a good laugh. When the resulting poems fail, as they often do, they teach us about what doesn't work, where the boundary lines are between the insightfully strange and the merely odd. When we get lucky, failures can dramatically illustrate the "click" between superficially unrelated ideas and how these sometimes offer illuminations that are difficult to discover when being more logical, straightforward or determined in our approach to poetry. The class or writing community may find it useful to compare interesting language from group poems with that found in poems written by individuals in the workshop. This is particularly valuable when the group is looking to integrate variety into the workshop/discussion of original poems.

Finally, there are other exercises in this section which ask us to share some writing experience together and explore its dynamics. These exercises simulate writers' friendships, café groups and other collaborations of intellect, art and productivity. Experienced writers know that we need each other: to bounce ideas off of, to share victories, and offer objective views of what we produce. This, in the long run, does not simply make our poems better: it makes them much better. Group work is a communal gift that artists have been sharing and practicing for centuries.

Our offerings here are just a beginning, a look at some of the possibilities of working together and alongside other writers.

❧ The Collaborative Poem

The Exercise

Each person begins with a separate piece of paper and writes her or his name at the bottom. At the top, write a line that interests you, preferably not a full sentence (so that the person after you has something to finish). Pass the paper to the person on your left, who then writes another line in response and folds the paper over so that only the new line is visible. The key is that every person in the group writing a line sees only the line written by the person before; no one sees the whole poem until the exercise is over. Try to keep things going by moving quickly, avoiding being too analytical: tap into the "id." Let your imagination go—as if you are a child running across a school yard.

Each writer, then, only reads a single line at a time, adds one, and hides the one before. Eventually the paper with your signature on it will return to you. When it does, write the final line, unfold the paper, and share the poem with the group.

This exercise is best done more than once, so people get comfortable with the process and the timing. Also after one round, the limits of obvious humor become clear and either get intensified or downplayed depending on the group.

Variation: Before starting, generate a list of 10-20 concrete words on the board or flip chart. Writers can use these words or not as they compose their lines.

Variation II: Use one of these group-generated poems as the basis of your revision process, making it more and more something you believe in. These are excellent examples for illustrating redundancies, unnecessary wordiness, and other issues of concision.

The Purpose

The process of this exercise dramatically shows how one line should impel the next, but as the results are shared poets will also sense how correspondences are created by repetition, tone, image, narrative, and other elements. Even if some of the wild stuff illustrates the merely weird, sometimes those lines become refrains of "going too far" and can be helpful when critiquing original works.

❧ The Cento
(* From the Latin for "patchwork," the cento is like a verbal collage.)

The Exercise

If you have passages from others' writing gathered in your Writer's Notebook, select and "stitch" them together into a unified whole. Don't change words or rearrange phrases within sentences, but cut words out, repeat, and arrange them to emphasize ideas and movements of feeling within the poem—whenever and however you desire. First pay attention to sequence and movement through your editing, then use the arrangement on the page to emphasize the shifts in feeling you are sensing. Like making a quilt, you should strive for creating a unified poem. Finally, be sure to credit the original writers by listing at the bottom of your creation their names and the works you quote.

The Purpose
Practicing the cento heightens our awareness of what Muriel Rukeyser calls "correspondences" among a variety of texts, along with the unities or contrasts, harmonies or ironies that move a poem along. These felt structures are sometimes easier to make use of if one is working with ready-made materials. The practice of the "cento" helps us learn movement, structure, and the choices of editing in a fluid or condensed fashion because we are sharpening our focus by borrowing the lines of others.

❧ The "Bad" Poem Exercise
(* This is a particularly good "ice breaker" for a poetry class or writing group.)

The Exercise
Write the names of ten everyday objects on the board. Choose any of these words and write a bad poem about it. The group gets to decide what makes a "bad poem." Afterward, share the poems and discuss what makes poems bad. Then, turn the discussion on its ear and talk about what makes poems good.

Variation: This exercise can also be framed as a contest that concludes with a vote regarding which poem is worst and which is the least successful as a "bad" poem. This variation focuses discussion on the "winning" poems, which in turn may enhance the inductive description of what makes poems good or bad that this exercise seeks to generate.

The Purpose
One idea here is to identify the many levels that weaken a poem's power or thwart its purpose. For those unused to the creative writing community, this is a "no-pressure" start, but the discussion should also reveal a good deal about poetry's assumptions and perspectives. Ironically, even poems that are deliberately awful can achieve exactly what they set out to do: make people laugh. So…are they so bad after all? The discussions of these nuances can illuminate our sense of poetry's ironies, debates and fluidity quite a bit.

❧ The Movie Maker

The Exercise
This one requires some preparation. The teacher or group leader needs to prepare index cards or slips of paper with the following directions on them:

- Begin with "To..."
- Total number of words: 6
- Begin with "This..."
- Use the phrase "...---, my friend,..."
- Begin with "And..."
- Ask a question
- Begin with an -ing word
- Mention something specific from nature
- Begin with "The..."
- Use "he"
- "Understood you" is the subject
- Use a proper name
- Total number of words: 4
- Mention a person's name
- Start with "I..."
- Begin with "From..."
- Mention a place name
- Use "she"
- Do not use "I"
- Describe an object

Put the cards in a hat so people can select one without seeing the directions. Writers should also have index cards or sheets of paper to write on.

Like the Collaborative Poem, this exercise has individuals contributing a single line to a group poem. Each person chooses a card and then writes a line on the blank sheet. It can be a complete sentence or not, but it shouldn't be exceedingly long.

Gather them up into one stack and have someone who reads aloud well read the results, in no particular order, as if they were a poem. Shuffle the deck and read again. Be sure to pay attention to the rhythm of the repeated phrase.

Variation I: Restrict directions on the cards or slips of paper to only grammatical ones and leave all content open.

Variation II: Mix in cards or slips to emphasize content: place names, names of people (famous or otherwise), and descriptions.

The Purpose
This is called "The Movie Maker" because one student remarked that the result of this exercise ended up feeling like a story because "he" and "she" started to seem like characters. What we also like about this exercise is that with all the randomness, the few repeated phrases and the repeated grammatical structures suggest a unity: getting a feel for the ways language can unify—rather than content alone—is essential for poets. This exercise also introduces phrasal repetition as a poetic device. The grammatical structure of a phrase can build rhythm, as in this example: "To the river overflowing its banks / From the Eastgate Mall / To the basement where my gym bag hangs." When it is the organizing structure of a poem, as it is in many of Walt Whitman's poems, it's called anaphoric verse.

Another purpose for this exercise is to provide material to practice revision. The drafts created are excellent for illustrating wordiness and other issues of word choice. They can also be used to practice revision as a matter of reordering, rearranging, and developing what is only skimmed, as well as removing unwanted material.

❧ The Prized Possession

The Exercise
Everyone in the class or writing group must bring a prized possession and anonymously place it on a table in the center of the room. The items must be small enough to fit into two hands. Everyone circles around, just looking at them, then choosing one. For a fixed period, write as if this object held great personal significance for you. Try for a mix of descriptive, narrative, and explanatory writing. Work these thoughts or observations into a poem.

Variation: Return to your own prized possession and allow it to "speak" its significance in the world. Write a first person poem, but it shouldn't be obvious that the speaker is an object.

The Purpose
This exercise helps us to experience the power of a symbol or emblem. When we talk about something having "sentimental value," we are referring to how a thing can evoke emotions, carry memories, and hold a relationship's story. The exercise asks writers to imagine a value in objects they don't own, stimulating the imagination. The hidden history or "back story" behind the possession must be inferred and imagined creatively by the individual writer.

❧ One-liners
(* This exercise requires either transparencies and pens or a bit of photocopying.)

The Exercise
Select any one of William Carlos Williams's short poems, like "The Term," "Poem" ("As the cat…"), "Nantucket," or "The Locust Tree in Flower." (Any short poem will do, although translations introduce problems). The teacher or group leader can either print the poem as a sentence on paper for groups or on an overhead for all to see.

Divide into small groups of three members each. If you use more than one sample poem, be sure pairs of groups deal with the same one in order to compare the results later. Each group must discuss the poem's movement and meaning, then break it into lines/stanzas to reinforce the ideas they've identified. Do not change or remove any words; simply arrange them on the page to reflect the content. Write on a transparency and display each group's choices. Discuss the various lines and their effects. Afterward, present and discuss the original version of the poem or poems.

The Purpose
Freed from the burden of working with original material, writers using this group exercise can explore the effects of line unit and line breaks on pacing, syntax, "flow," and other movement within the poem. This exercise isolates the decision about lines, stanzas, and thought units (like

prepositional phrases or modifier-noun phrases) to get a feeling for how line length and line breaks can emphasize single words, images, or concepts. Finally, it introduces the idea of the line break as either a block or an aid to quick comprehension, as obstacle or amplifier of fluid motion. The line is a fundamental component of the craft that poets use to invite the reader's attention to particular moments in a poem.

❧ The Line Break as Pause
—after Denise Levertov

(* For this exercise, you will need to do a bit of preparation. Look through your Writer's Notebook for a prose passage that has poetic potential—however you define it. Type it, as prose, and be ready to read it aloud: if you're unwilling to share or change it, select a different passage. Prepare three copies to bring to the class or group.)

The Exercise

In groups of three, each writer will read his or her passage aloud as the other two follow along with their own copies. As you read yours, go slowly but not ploddingly, paying attention to rhythm and emphasis.

While you are reading, the group members who are listening will mark their copies of your passage, paying attention to your pauses—particularly non-punctuated ones. All members read the piece again on their own, putting a slash (/) in for small pauses and a double slash (//) for longer ones. Compare your notation, then read the passage again, imagining a line break for the single slashes and a stanza break for double slashes. If you end up with stanzas at the ends of all sentences and/or line breaks that are all end-stopped, then re-read the poem paying attention to all pauses *within* lines, noting them with a slash.

Discuss the differences between the versions each member comes up with (or different ways group members would read parts), then move on to the prose passage of the next member and repeat the exercise until all work has been covered.

After the exercise, rewrite your passage with line breaks and stanzas. Now consider the units you have created with your pausing, try to feel where the reader's attention is drawn as a result of these pauses and breaks. Since punctuation already creates its own hesitation, try a version where the punctuation falls within a line and the breaks come at the slashes.

The Purpose

Practicing "The Line Break as Pause" helps us experience both the grammatical and non-grammatical pauses in a piece of writing and gives us practice in using them (or not!) as the basis for line breaks. It has the dual advantage of providing practice/discussion regarding line breaks and demonstrating one method for converting prose into poetry.

❦ Five Senses

(* There is a version of this exercise for individual writers in Chapter Four.)

The Exercise

In groups of five or fewer, brainstorm a short list of random but interesting objects or places. Pick one as a group, then each member writes a description/impression of the object that begins from the vantage point of one of the senses. Feel free to allow your object or place to "spin-off" into other directions or areas that spring to mind as you are writing. Read the sections you have produced in any random order, then discuss how well the collaboration works and what changes you might make to improve the flow and coordinate the ideas. At this point, play with the order of the individual sections to see which one produces the best results.

Variation: Like the Collaborative Poem, each writer puts down one part then passes to the left so the next person can add to it. The whole group deals with the same triggering object or place and all work from the same sense for one round. For example, everyone might write down the aspects of a public pool. The first person records sound, passes the paper; the second person writes from tactile feeling, passes the paper; the third writes from sight, and so on. You can also agree to write in completely separate sections or strive to continue from the section before.

The Purpose

This is an exercise, adapted from the definition of a poetic "image"—that is, something which appeals to one or more of the five physical senses. It also introduces the senses as a starting point in generating a collaborative poem and providing its structure, and it illustrates how a poem is amplified by a variety of sensual perspectives. Finally, Five Senses demonstrates how sensory perceptions sometimes act as a catalyst and spin the writer off into unanticipated directions.

❦ Writing Off the Music

(* The teacher, group leader, or individual members select instrumental music. It helps if the pieces are a little out of the ordinary but not bombastic. We've successfully used Paul Winter with various world instruments and environmental/animal sounds and Peter Gabriel's soundtrack to *The Last Temptation of Christ*.)

The Exercise

Have everyone listen to a piece of music once with eyes closed. Then, on a second hearing write where the music took you. Compose a poem of your visions.

Usually, when we do this in groups, we take about 10 minutes to write in any way each person needs to after the second listening. That writing can become the basis of revision, first using methods from Found Poems and Line Break as Pause. These drafts can be shared with the group afterward or not, depending on the mood.

The Purpose

Tapping into the suggestive quality of instrumental music can evoke interior images or narratives. In this exercise we seek to enjoy these and to use them as the content of a poem. It is also instructive to experience how wordless art can create such impressions or arouse emotions, helping to emphasize that concrete, specific images and rhythmic language can evoke far beyond what they declare.

❧ How Do You Mean "Cleave"? (Group Version)

(* Unlike the earlier version of this exercise, this group activity is set up as a game. Done early on in a class or group's history, it can be a great ice-breaker, too.)

The Exercise

Version I: The group leader or teacher must prepare a pile of index cards labeled with words with a variety of meanings, like *finish, jump, shoot, deck, file, ram, pen, rail,* etc., one word per card. Each word must be on two cards. Divide the group into four smaller teams. Two teams face each other, are given the same word. In a set amount of time, say 3-5 minutes, each team must generate as many definitions as possible including official, slang, specialized, and idiomatic uses. Rules must be established beforehand regarding homophones and variations in form. At the end of the time limit, compare lists, crossing off any that overlap, and awarding points for the ones that differ. The other two teams must act as judges, with the teacher/group leader as final arbitrator.

Version II: This is the more extended version, where the generation of the lists is a part of the game. Teams are given a set amount of time to create a list of as many multiple-meaning words as they can, with definitions (as above). At the end of the time, lists of a set number (3? 5?) are copied without definitions. One list of words at a time is delivered to the opposing team, who must create definitions in a set amount of time. If the opposing team matches or exceeds the number originally created, they gain points. Each exchanged list counts as one round. The teacher or group leader is the judge in all disputes. Points, awards, and penalties should be established beforehand.

Variation: Construct poems that integrate many of these versatile words into them—so that readers have to keep moving, the piece unfolding as the context reveals which meaning is intended.

The Purpose

This exercise helps us experience how words exist in a matrix of meanings and uses that we recognize in context, and it aids us in claiming for ourselves a wider range of that network in a single usage. It also reinforces what we might call the social character of the writing process. This character is essential for building the workshop community, if that is where the group is bound. The experience of a game atmosphere embodies the delight in form, in rules and parameters that enable freedom (an analog for poetic pleasure in many ways).

❧ One-a-Day Poems
—adapted from Deborah Austin

The Exercise
Version I: The group leader or teacher selects a contemporary poem, usually not from the anthology used for class. The selection can be based on the lesson at hand, on a poet to introduce, or simply on personal favorites. Put the writer's name and the title of the poem on the board or flipchart; the class or group has a sheet of paper on which they copy this heading.

The poem is read once for the overall sense and movement. Then as it is read again, listeners try to hold onto particular words or phrases without taking notes. Once the reading is done, listeners write the phrases they recall then respond to the poem: what they liked or didn't, what it made them think about, or how it made them feel.

Version II: Using selections from The Poem Purchase, the person who selected the piece reads it using the directions above.

Version III: As an initiation to workshop (responding to others' poems), teacher or group leader reads a student poem aloud. Depending on the temper of the group or its evolution, it can be done anonymously or not. Listeners respond as above.

Version IV: Using a student's poem, the teacher or group leader reads as outlined above. The listeners begin responding to the poem by identifying what are its major strengths; then, they can offer suggestions for improvement. These are collected and delivered to the writer. The anonymity of the writer and of individual respondents is up to the group to choose.

The Purpose
This exercise helps to create a poetry-rich environment using what are often fine models as it introduces new poets and different types of poetry to the class or group. It also emphasizes poetry's aural quality by developing listening and memory skills. If the latter versions are used, this exercise introduces the workshop method in a quicker, less intense format by focusing on readers' reactions to a student's work, rather than on the writer's intentions.

❧ A Painting in Three Levels
(* Just as with Writing Off the Music, artwork will have to be selected and provided to the group. Realistic styles work far better than abstract paintings, but trying a variety is always interesting.)

The Exercise
Using the same painting, everyone responds by writing a strictly descriptive sketch, leaves a few spaces and makes an asterisk. Then everyone writes a narrative, a quick story of what's happening in this scene, even extending to the preceding action that sets this moment up or to the ensuing action. Again, everyone leaves a few spaces and draws an asterisk. Finally, everyone

responds to the art by articulating what it makes you think about, how it makes you feel, what it reminds you of, etc.

Share the results to discuss the differences in the three approaches and to uncover the variety of personal responses.

The Purpose
The vocabulary and structures of these different modes of writing (descriptive, narrative, and explanatory) can be very different in their qualities and effects, so this exercise separates them into distinct sections. In addition to delineating these modes, this exercise introduces the visual arts as a springboard for our writing.

Section Two: Writing Poems

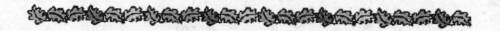

Chapter Three

Generate a Poem

Although many of the exercises presented earlier in this book have invited us to write poems, we now turn our attention to exercises that generate at least one draft of a poem per activity. Certainly, many of these can be taken on by members of a creative writing class or a writer's group and the resulting poem drafts can be shared and discussed, but the design in this section and the one that follows it is toward individual work.

Sitting down to write a poem is legendary for its daunting quality. Much has been made of the difficulty and the challenge that a blank page represents. Experienced writers, however, have often found ways to create an atmosphere conducive to creativity and poetry writing. For some, this involves particular times of the day or specific places; for others, it means following habits; but for a large number of us it means practicing a discipline of readiness and availability. We encourage you to experiment in order to learn about your own sensibilities and get the most out your time. We present a number of these techniques here.

As you work through these exercises, keep in mind our primary goal: developing good, habitual writers and poets. We hope these activities help you to shape your life and make room for creative work, develop habits of mind and heart that invite your subjects. Also keep in mind that we present these exercises to help you produce good drafts of poems, not necessarily finished poems. Toward that end, don't be afraid to take risks, to write and think in ways that may be unusual, unexpected, or even "untrue" in terms of your feelings. Trying on emotions in a creative writing exercise is one way of challenging ourselves, thinking about things, and increasing our own capacity for self-understanding. Contrast may be the best way to define our true awareness because of the challenge it presents to that knowledge. If we stick to habitual ways of thinking we sometimes cut ourselves off from the possibility of discovering something new, even about ourselves.

There should be something in the exercises in this and the following section for everyone in terms of interests and areas of greater potential for creative exploration. Many times, students and workshop members have commented on how they started an exercise convinced that it wouldn't go anywhere, only to be startled by what emerged.

❧ Responding to Art

(* This exercise is similar to "Writing Off the Music," but it uses visual and graphic art to generate the writing.)

The Exercise
Go to a museum or any place where you can see a number of different pieces of art: paintings, sculpture, photography, and so on. Pick one that you find moving or affecting. Now write a poem about this piece. Consider the possibilities of putting this piece of art into words. You can write to it, about it, or from it. Try several of these until you get to your original impression or something better.

If the class or writers group goes together, after you have finished share your drafts with the others while standing in front of the piece of art that inspired your writing.

(Of course, this exercise can be done surfing the Internet or browsing through the library for artwork; the atmosphere of a museum is part of the experience, though, so the "travel" version of this exercise is often better.)

Variations: Write a poem from the perspective of the artist who created the piece. What was she/he thinking? Why? Or write a poem from the perspective of characters or objects portrayed in the artwork, or from the work of art itself, and so on. A work of art that really "speaks" to us can result in a whole series of poems from the many perspectives of these variations.

The Purpose
Responding to Art taps into the energy that sometimes flows from one work of art to another. Professional artists have used this technique for centuries, often making art that has been inspired by other works—sometimes from the same genre, sometimes from a different one. There is even a specific Greek word for poems based on other artwork: *ekphrasis*. As we experience how others approach this exercise, through sharing our drafts, we can explore the larger range of options for responding to art in original, personal ways. Many museums have produced books of ekphrastic poetry, but we can also find many other examples. Denise Levertov wrote quite a number of poems responding to paintings, including "The Book Without Words" (Anselm Keifer), while William Carlos Williams wrote about many of Pieter Brueghel's works; John Haines responds to Michelangelo, Vincent Van Gogh, Edward Hopper, and others.

❧ Image Electricity

The Exercise
Write a poem about your feelings, but use no images; in other words, compose your poem in statements. On a separate sheet of paper try to come up with images or actions, ones you haven't seen before in print, that *show* the feelings you have written in your first draft. See how these changes refocus the poem's character. (An example might be the statement "I'm sad over the death of my grandmother" being written as the image "My grandmother's useless cane leans against a dying oak."

The Purpose

This exercise is the poetic version of Mary Shelley's great fictional experiment, where we try to bring life to lifeless things. Basic, generic statements cannot be visualized, so we need to return to the experiences they represent and more fully imagine them. Doing so helps create images that amplify our feelings, thoughts or ideas. Hopefully, we experience the rich complexity inherent in sensory language, which is often more powerful than statements in producing strong, evocative poems that retain a sense of mystery. It also provides practice in coming up with images that are fresh or original.

❧ The Prose Poem

The Exercise

In a paragraph or two—no longer than a page—write a poem that uses the rhythm of the sentence rather than the line as its guiding movement. It can be a story, a description, a mood captured. Each word must contribute to the overall effect still, so take some practice at eliminating all unnecessary words, phrases, and clauses. Try to develop images rather than only stating the nature of things.

The Purpose

This exercise deliberately blurs the lines between two literary genres, poetry and prose. Almost all successful contemporary writers of poetry have written a few of these; a number of writers have penned large numbers of them. The effect we are all looking for here is a "hybrid" that celebrates the best qualities of both genres. At its best, the Prose Poem creates a hybrid poetic space that can sometimes accommodate ideas, thoughts, stories and language that do not work as well in other forms.

❧ Who Will You Become?

The Exercise

Imagine yourself in ten, twenty, or thirty years. What are the habitual places or everyday activities of this person-you'll-be? Write a poem from the perspective of the person you think you will become; make it about something that has become important to "that person." Think both inside and outside the "square," and make your futuristic vision of yourself a challenging one. These poem drafts can be monologues or third person points of view.

Variation I: Consider choices you've already made that have rendered certain futures for yourself unlikely. Project how your life would have evolved had you gone down another path. How would you—your world-view or your personality—be different? Now imagine this person in a particular, typical place at a specific time. Is she stuck in commuter traffic with snow beginning to fall? Is he sitting at the kitchen table, in the dead of night—again!—wondering if the phone will ring with bad news? Write a poem from that person's point of view about something that's become important to him or her, trying to work in the sensory details from that place and time you've imagined.

Variation II: Like the exercise, An Epistle, compose a poem that is a letter, but in this case write a poem addressing an earlier version of yourself from your current point of view. Fully imagine a moment of crisis or decision or strong emotion so you can refer to the particular details of that instant. It should not be clear that the "I" and the "you" in the poem are the same person.

The Purpose
"Who Will you Become" focuses, in a roundabout way, on the moments of crossing, providing an opportunity to speak from or about those crucial times. A secondary goal of such exercises is to gain a greater understanding of the choices and consequences of our decisions. The idea of who or what we may become is really an exercise in understanding our present state of mind, our fears and our wishes.

❧ The "First"
(* This exercise requires a copy of a Wendell Berry poem or something similar.)

The Exercise
Read Wendell Berry's poem "The First." (Lisel Mueller's "Tears" also works well.) Now, brainstorm common, physical experiences. These should be specific and bodily. Develop a list of five to ten. Next, imagine you are the first human being to experience this. What are the sensory aspects? What possible conclusions could the first person to live through this come to? Draft poems that fill in the sentence, "The first woman who..." and "The first man who..." Write a brief poem about one such ordinary (or extraordinary!) action.

The Purpose
This is an exercise in what our friend Wayne Dodd calls "remembering things correctly." It seeks to awaken the original amazement of sensations that we've grown used to, and to remind ourselves and readers of such feelings and their power as primal experiences. Recovering the "newness" of an experience is not easy, but we also have the flexibility to either imagine as near to the truth as possible or to see things partly from our new vantage point and thus view them "correctly." How we interpret "correctness," of course, is up to us and part of the journey of discovery the exercise indicates.

❧ Writing a Portrait

The Exercise
Using the Memory Storehouse exercise or some current reflection, identify people who arouse strong feelings in you. Imagine individual people in a specific setting, as if sitting for a portrait, or in a moment that captures the essence of that person, as if in a photograph. Brainstorm about several people.

Select a subject, and write his or her portrait. In describing your subject, capture that person's distinctive spirit. When painters compose a portrait, they frequently are not seeking a photographically realistic or representational version of the person's appearance. They hope to capture some sense of the subject's essential quality, her or his personality or way of being.

Variation: Having fully imagined this person, try storytelling or allow him or her to speak in the first-person.

The Purpose
This exercise hopes to evoke the complexity of a person in a kind of word drawing, and to help writers experience and experiment with the numerous ways of doing so. Portraiture, after all, can be detailed or sketchy; flippant or serious; absurd and nonrepresentational or staid and dark (see Edwin Arlington Robinson's "Richard Cory").

❧ Eavesdropping on the Music
(* This exercise is both easily adaptable and recommended as a group activity.)

The Exercise
Take your Writer's Notebook to a public place—dining hall or restaurant, gym or health center, post office, etc.—and listen to people's conversations. Jot down expressions or exchanges that are interesting. Listen to the music of everyday speech, the tone of speakers, and the vividness of their language. Next try to assemble these into a poem, either with a single speaker or many, using the same guidelines as the Cento (see Section I).

The Purpose
"Eavesdropping" in this way lets us listen to spoken language and appreciate its poetic and distinctive rhythms. Another benefit is that engaging in this exercise heightens awareness of our own idiosyncratic rhythms and phrasings in order to discover their musical or poetic qualities. Sometimes we can tell who's called out to us by the way they say, "Hey" or "Hi" or "Hello." This uniqueness is a matter of tone, timbre, and pacing—all elements of music and poetry. For poets, the way people phrase things is also part of the remarkable power of language. Shifts in phrasings and rhythms can signal changes in emotion in a conversation and in a poem, so we must focus our attention by eavesdropping. Many of e.e. cummings' poems rely on spoken phrasing for their rhythm; see his poem beginning "raise the shade/will youse dearie?" or "nobody loses all the time" or "my sweet old etcetera."

❧ The Epistle

The Exercise
Write a poem that is a letter to someone it is difficult or impossible to communicate with, perhaps someone who has died or a famous person or one who does not yet exist. You might consult your Memory Storehouse lists.

Be sure to compose the poem as if it is a poem and not an actual letter. The tone will be different from that of a letter yet possess some formal similarities—keeping this in mind may help with the exercise.

The Purpose
We have had great success with The Epistle, probably because of its liberating quality. This is an exercise in speculation, memory, or alleviating frustration—all through the vehicle of the letter. The intimate tone of a letter gives the poem generated from this exercise an unusual, often memorable quality. The Epistle is one of our "standards": an exercise that may be returned to over time and still produce dramatic effects, good poems, and high quality reflections.

❧ Mythology Forward
(* Consulting Joseph Campbell's many writings on the subject of mythology is a plus here, as his discussion of what makes myths enduring and magical is a formidable achievement.)

The Exercise
Pick a character out of mythology, fairy tales, or some similar genre. Put that character's name at the top of the page. Now write a poem about a modern person who seems to have some connection to the myth. One example of this exercise is a poem I once saw titled "Ulysses and Penelope" that was actually written about a truck driver and a waitress. "Hercules" could, in this context, be a poem about a janitor; "Gretel," a poem about a runaway teenager; and so on.

The Purpose
By drawing parallels between contemporary figures and characters that inhabit mythology, we say something about the enduring quality of the human condition, of our gifts and our troubles. This is an exercise that attempts to borrow something from the power of myth and transfer that energy to a contemporary scene, figure, action or place. The Oxford University Press anthology *Gods and Mortals: Modern Poems on Classical Myths,* edited by Nina Kossman, was published in 2001 and provides good models of some of the many ways poets have reinvented such ancient stories.

❧ Small Research Nature Poem
(* This exercise might be preceded by some time spent outdoors, particularly at unusual times of day, night, or season—this may stimulate or awaken interesting memories of the natural world.)

The Exercise
Think about a time in your life when nature impressed you. Then go to the library and do some quick research on the aspect of nature you are thinking of: the weather, a place, a specific animal, event, etc. Pay particular attention to the language you are discovering in your research: look for interesting or musical words you would like to use in a poem about nature. You may stop your research when you have learned a few things you didn't know before about your subject. Finally, write a draft of a poem about your memory and try to utilize some of the new information or language from your research.

Variation: Do the research, but don't rely on memory. Instead, go out and try to experience the natural event or space. Being alone may be productive here, but it is not necessary. Take your Writer's Notebook and write down your impressions and your thoughts. Compose a poem based on your notes, expanding on them and taking the poem into new directions when you see or feel an opportunity to do so.

The Purpose
One of the wonders of learning about nature is found in discovering its complexity and its language. Nature's encyclopedia is broad and deep. Storms, plants, mountains, desert life, sea birds, all of these are fascinating in their own right, but the language, the words associated with them are often just as remarkable. When we generate poems out of research in and about nature, we create wonderful opportunities to observe, philosophize and compare—and we create the opportunity to use words and colors we have not used before. Since every area of human endeavor has its own vocabulary, this exercise illustrates the variegated tones available to poets who blend specialized language with other forms. See Pattiann Rogers' poems for powerful examples of these strategies.

❧ The Poem You Can't Forget

The Exercise
Write a descriptive poem about something you've seen that you can't forget. Try to learn something new about this event or to discover why it is exactly that the event is so compelling, what people can learn from it, etc. Some candidates for poem subjects may be listed in your Memory Storehouse already.

Variation: This exercise produces dramatic accounts of traffic accidents, near-death experiences, and more. But remember that some unforgettable things may be humorous as well. Try this exercise with humorous moments and memories. See Naomi Shihab Nye's poem "Alarm Clock" or Richard Garcia's "Why I Left the Church" for good examples of how this may be done.

The Purpose
All of us witness remarkable, shocking or amazing things from time to time. We use this exercise to tap events we may have seen by the roadside, on a city street, in the home, in the desert or on the ocean, and turn them into moments of deep reflection, learning and poetry. Poems generated by this exercise are also good opportunities to try to "say the unsayable": to try to find the words to describe and understand remarkable, unforgettable things.

❧ Poem in Three Levels

(* We first encountered this exercise in Wayne Dodd's creative writing courses at Ohio University and have used it regularly in our own classes ever since.)

The Exercise

1) Place a few interesting objects on a table. (We have used pine cones, leaves, a pack of cigarettes, house keys, lipstick—whatever is handy—but let your imaginations roam in the selection of objects to use). Choose one of the objects and write a stanza about it. Put an asterisk below this writing.

2) Next, write a stanza about your parents. When it is finished, put an asterisk below.

3) Finally, write a stanza about yourself. Polish all three stanzas making any adjustments you can think of toward helping them work together as a poem.

The Purpose

This exercise moves our reflections and our writing from the outside world inward   toward the self. It challenges us to create or discover connections between the three layers. More importantly, perhaps, this exercise demonstrates how poems may leap from one level, perspective or subject to another and sometimes seek out their own connections in interesting and non-linear ways. The poet David Mura is fond of telling his students to never develop a poem "in a straight line." We can leap from perspective to perspective (or from other aspects in the poem) and create wonderful tensions, connections and journeys.

❧ The Thing Poem

(* Where the Image Album restricts the description to the visual observation, this exercise requires a more expanded sensory participation.)

The Exercise

Observe an object or living thing using all of your senses. Try free-writing your sensations and impressions when doing so, either one sense at a time or all at once using alternating periods of observation and freewriting.

Draft a poem that integrates many aspects of both the subject and the sensations the subject creates—paying attention to how the sounds and rhythms of your language contribute to the mood of the poem. Experiment with moving from one mood to another (and perhaps to a third!) occasionally returning to the initial mood. After detailing the object fairly objectively, allow the poem to leap inward toward whatever lies waiting to be discovered there.

The Purpose

Concentrating on a single object allows the details there to suggest meanings. Poems are often a rich complex of emotions rather than a single one: by isolating one's subject (in this case, the "thing") we can allow this effect to emerge. The Thing Poem also uses the objective world as a kind of template for the subjective. Perception in poetry is often a blend of the two states: observed and observer. Many of Robert Bly's poems employ this dynamic; see his prose poems "A Caterpillar" or "A Bouquet of Ten Roses."

❧ The Found Poem

(* If you haven't been collecting passages from your reading in your Writer's Notebook, you'll need to go in search of a prose selection with vivid description, evocative imagery, and/or remarkable language.)

The Exercise

Choose one passage from one prose text that impresses you. Arrange it into lines and stanzas to heighten the poetic effect you may have sensed in the prose. You can omit words or whole phrases but not rearrange them. You can repeat phrases or words but not change any words. Use line length, line break, spaces within and around lines, stanzas, and any other arrangements on the page.

Give your poem a title, then create an epigraph between the title and the body of the poem that says "A Found Poem of …" and give the title of the original and the author.

The Purpose

Found poems can illuminate the poetry hidden in language that is not presented in a poetic context. Often, the found poem intensifies—or contradicts by irony or sarcasm—the poetic intentions of an original piece, as it does in Denise Levertov's "News Report, September 1991" from a *New York Times* article or in Raymond Carver's found poems in *A New Path to the Waterfalls* from the stories of Anton Chekhov. Below these goals, this exercise also intends to give voice or context to the effects poetic elements have in language that is not calling attention to itself *as* poetry. Borrowing these interesting passages also gives us further practice in all of the other techniques used in creating a good poem: line breaks, stanza breaks, pacing, diction, tone, etc.

❧ The Poem Buyout

—adapted from Beth Bentley's exercise

(* If you haven't done The Poem Purchase exercise yet, follow those directions first. If you have completed The Poem Purchase or Constructing an Anthology, use one of your selections from either of those exercises here.)

The Exercise

Having "purchased" the poem, you now make it completely yours by writing a poem that emulates the style and even the strategy of the sample poem. You may need to map the sections of the poem, noting shifts in topic as well as tone in order to imitate its movement. Try to adapt the poem's technique or form to something more fitting of your life, more true to your experience and knowledge. (Victor Hernandez Cruz's well known "Problems with Hurricanes"—a poem about the dangers of hurricane-force winds turning simple objects into missiles— might become "Problems with Mudslides," "Problems with Empty Factories" or "Problems with Tornadoes" in your hands.)

If you stick closely to the original poem, be sure to credit the original in the title or body of your poem, or you can create an epigraph saying "After Victor Hernandez Cruz" or "After 'The Problem with Hurricanes'."

Variation I: Respond to your sample poem. In other words, answer your sample poem's central argument, perhaps even addressing the poet directly (this works best, as you might imagine, if you disagree with the original's intent.)

Variation II: Turn the poem around: if the speaker is male, re-invent the poem's situation from a woman's point of view and write that poem in her voice. Consider shifting race, economic class, sexual orientation, political stance, nationality, moral or religious belief, and so on.

The Purpose
In addition to including most of the benefits delineated in the original exercise, "The Poem Purchase," this version transfers the energy of active reading to writing—propelling our own work from the gravity of another's. This also helps us internalize the structures of poems, expands our own repertoire of poem-shapes, and provides models for movement with poems that we may not have developed if left to our own devices.

❧ Writing "Off the Subject"

The Exercise
Pick a subject that you feel really passionate about, anything at all as long as the feeling you get when thinking about it is strong. Write the name of that subject at the top of a sheet of paper. Next, think of an original and fitting metaphor for your subject. You must pick a metaphor that is unusual, one that you have not seen before. For example, if love is your subject, your metaphor might be a mailbox, a train, or a refrigerator—and so on.

The next step is to write a poem about the metaphor, i.e. a poem about the mailbox, train, or fridge. Keep in mind when you are writing the poem that you are secretly talking about your original subject, but stay focused on the metaphor (mailbox, train, etc.) When you finish the poem, cross out the subject word you originally put at the top of the page and replace it with the metaphor as the title. Here is an example:

> **Refrigerator**
>
> The way you hum disturbs me.
> Late at night, when my throat is dry
> all I can think of is you.
> But it's hard to leave warmth
> behind and move toward something
> so distant, so many obstacles in the dark
> between us. Sometimes
> I dream I've left the sheets
> and am walking the floor.

I can't see my legs as I wander.
When I open this door
what will I find?

The Purpose
Creating a single metaphor that suggests a fresh view of the subject can generate tones or colors that we might otherwise not have chosen or seen. The idea here is not to create a "secret code poem" no one will understand, but rather to create a new way of looking at subjects that readers will see clearly and understand while at the same time allowing for complexity not initially conceived of.

Short-line Railroad

The Exercise
Consult your Image Album for brief descriptions or develop a series of new ones, whatever comes to mind—things you've seen that day, that week, that month, that year. Begin with a number of short images on a piece of paper. Collect as many of them as you can; then cull the images 1) into groups that seem to make sense or 2) into groups that make no sense at all.

Write a poem using very short lines trying to make connections between your images.

The Purpose
Forcing ourselves into poems made of shorter lines limits certain choices—and sometimes acts as a refining agent inside our writing. The two possible versions—where the images are either logical or nonsensical—provide two very different frameworks for organizing imagery into a poem. The first provides the coherent sequence or connective material, say the "rails" and "ties," while the second creates a challenge to the reader to supply the unifying element(s) by presenting only the "stations."

The Cemetery Poem

The Exercise
Visit a local cemetery and wander around a bit. Take note of graves that catch your imagination by recording the name, inscriptions, dates, and any details about the physical layout or area. Gather a few groups of these notes, and if you can, collect further information about the graveyard or some of the people buried there from the local library, church, temple or newspaper. Now, compose a poem about the cemetery itself. (Consider Henry Wadsworth Longfellow's "The Jewish Cemetery at Newport" or Robert Lowell's "For the Union Dead" or Allen Tate's "Ode to the Confederate Dead.")

Variation I: Compose a poem about the people whose graves caught your imagination, either writing about them or in the deceased person's voice. (Consider the many poems from *Spoon*

River Anthology by Edgar Lee Masters or the dark portraits of the residents of Tilbury Town by Edgar Arlington Robinson.)

The Purpose
This exercise presents a ready-made subject with infinite variation by tapping into the emotional experience of visiting a burial ground. Grand themes of life, death, memory, loss, absence, beauty, and forgetting, often present themselves in this exercise as well as the challenge of allowing conflicting emotions into in a single poem.

❧ Conversation in a Long Line

The Exercise
Begin writing about something you're interested in getting down, a story perhaps, or a scene (avoid a stream-of-consciousness free-write based in the impressions of the moment, though). You can write any way you want to, as long as the tone is conversational. But as you go, don't be afraid to experiment by saying something unusual. The streets in your scene might pick themselves up and lie themselves down again at different times of the day, for example; the characters in your story could have secret identities or change gender halfway through; and so on. Let strange things enter the poem and break up the narrative (or the monotony) when the poem seems to need it. Try for a balance between the mundane and the unusual, perhaps even between the literal truth and the imagined additions.

Once done with a first draft, write the poem in long lines, two lines per stanza, with an indentation of a couple of spaces for the second line of each stanza. Craft your poem a bit by eliminating wordiness but retaining the conversational tone—by sharpening the narrative but retaining the imaginative departures, and by honing the lines and line breaks but retaining the stretch and inclusiveness of a long line. Of course, add or delete lines as you see fit but retain the couplets.

The Purpose
This exercise challenges us to take conversational tone—and the long line that suits it—to a different level, so that it is compelling and capable of surprise. The purpose here is to open our aesthetic sensibilities to the borderlines where the merely conversational crosses over and becomes poetry. Using this border effectively can create power in poems because it redefines what we mean by "poetic language." Perhaps the best practitioner of this type of poetry is C.K Williams; see his books *Tar, With Ignorance* or *Selected Poems*.

❧ From the News

The Exercise
If you've been collecting newspaper articles in your Writer's Notebook, use one of those; if not, scan a variety of newspapers—*New York Times, News of the Weird*, or even *The Enquirer* or *The Star*—and select a few stories that move you.

Write a poem in the voice of one of the people involved in one of the items but do not touch upon the incident itself. Instead, consider a moment in the past that held the first seed of what resulted in the story.

Variation: Write a poem in the voice of a family member held in or caught by a decisive moment involving the person in the story. The speaker must be struggling to choose, but you don't need to indicate his or her decision.

The Purpose
News stories, even strange ones, can sometimes generate an emotional nexus or atmosphere to write from, one that poets who rely on personal experience may overlook. This exercise also focuses on persona and/or monologue, both fruitful poetic techniques, but also ones that require stretching the imagination to a full character, rather than an incident. Read any of Ai's poems in *Vice: New and Selected Poems.*

❧ Book/Cover

The Exercise
Brainstorm a list of characters with improbable roles, jobs, or situations—like *the anorexic delivery person* or *the bar bouncer who is a recovering alcoholic.* Beware of stereotypes and stock characters, like the prostitute with the heart of gold or the mobster who is a loving family man. Strive for everyday people who embody their own contradictions.

Now, write a poem in this person's voice being faithful to his or her particular human struggle, rather than the clarity of your outside view.

The Purpose
Because the speaker is divided internally, the premise for this exercise explores the narrative possibilities (or the tension) between a character and the full integrity of that character's voice. It also illustrates how all poems are voiced in some way, even if the "character" is an aspect of ourselves; thus, this exercise opens up to the possibility of considering our own contradictions as well.

❧ Writing the Blues

The Exercise
Put the name of a color at the center of a paper, then brainstorm all your associations with that color. For example, Green might suggest envy, Spring, new life, possibility, inexperience, the political party, grass, money, and people you know with that name as well as their personalities.

Write a poem using a range of these associations, personifying the color. The title should be ambiguous, like "Black History."

The Purpose

Integrating multiple meanings of a single word with the creation of character, this exercise invites us to consider and connect layers of meaning in a single word as it expands and contrasts in definition and association. Exercises such as this one can easily move beyond "word play" when we reflect deeply about seemingly haphazard associations; they also challenge us to create the "poetry world," (like the one made up of cartoons in certain cinematic explorations) where the assumption is that everything matters inside words themselves.

American Haiku

(* Typically, haiku are short poems in three lines of 5, 7, and 5 syllables each—and expressing a moment of illumination through a nature image. But in the American version, feel free to let your subjects wander a bit, without abandoning the "illumination is happening right now" idea.)

The Exercise

Write a poem in three lines of approximately of 5, 7, and 5 syllables each. Try to capture some moment in nature (or elsewhere) that seems important and helps us to understand something more completely. Still strive to capture the concrete sensory detail of the moments that seem "lit from within" because these are particularly well suited subjects for haiku. Put yourself in a frame of mind that is open to the immediacy of things around you—observe, don't think!—and see what surfaces in terms of the poem.

Variation: Gary Snyder has used the haiku structure as the organizing principle in longer poems, which he calls "Hitched Haiku" in *The Back Country;* see also his "Little Songs for Gaia" in *Axehandles.*

The Purpose

The goal of haiku is a moment of "illumination," a small but highly lit, potent, and alive picture that we can enjoy and learn from. This verse also embodies the idea of poetic form in the way that, traditionally, haiku have brief observations set up like two poles while the reader's imagination provides the energy that arcs between them. Because these two observations are often physically observable details, this exercise encourages us to suggest rather than declare, to present images rather than conclusions.

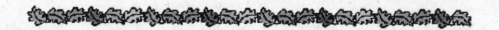

Chapter Four

Advanced Exercises

Of course, writing a poem well is always challenging, so the relative difficulty of any of these exercises may seem negligible at times, depending on the approach you take. In this section, however, we present activities that "push" in different ways from those presented earlier. They are "advanced" in this way: they are an extension into different challenges, more complex at times, perhaps, and more refined in their goals. Writing is a challenge and a problem, a task that probably eludes as often as it satisfies us. In this section we hope to keep the train going and pick up the speed. But in any event, we are satisfied if we keep you moving on for a bit in the hope that there are many pastures yet to be found and admired, many places and ideas yet to explore and learn from, many ways that art can come alive in us that we have not yet seen.

Our experience strongly suggests that engaging any artistic task over a long period of time requires focus, but it also thrives when we discover new ways and techniques in order to keep the activity fresh and interesting. But the real challenge and the true barometer of our needs as writers is a question, often an intuition, that only we can answer. It is always personal; it is always necessary. We present these exercises as further queries and options to explore, one more part of a long-term strategy of development. We hope they lead you to ways to renew yourself as you develop greater skill and more lively perception.

❧ Five Senses

(* This is an individualized version of the group exercise we outlined earlier.)

The Exercise

Write a poem in five sections, one section for each of the individual physical senses: sight, hearing, scent, taste, and touch. Begin each section with an image that strongly evokes the physical sense you are concentrating on, but you don't have to stay with that sense alone. Just make sure you return to the primary sense often. Also, connections between the sections do not have to be direct or literal. In other words, feel free to follow impressions and intuitions rather than being logical and orderly. Revise and polish this one a few times for clarity of imagery and cohesiveness.

The Purpose

The poetic image is by definition something that evokes one or more of the five senses. This exercise uses that convention as a way of practicing all of the senses in a single stroke, as broad a view of imagery as we can muster. At the same time, its use of the five senses as an organizing principle encourages us to think through those as a way of exploring interesting connections between subjects.

❧ Notes on the Pillow

The Exercise

Write a poem that is designed to be left on someone's pillow (quite an intimate act!). The note writer must be a character, not the poet. Is it a love note? An apology? From a baby sitter? A thief? For an added challenge, try to construct the poem so that the note-writer says all the right things, but there is something in *how* things are expressed that makes the reader suspect insincerity or complications beneath the simplified surface. The note-writer does not intend to express these complications, so they must be subtle.

The Purpose

This framed exercise proceeds from a dramatic moment and demonstrates how poems can evolve out of such moments. It also relies heavily on voice and persona as a way of exploring the mystery and perhaps amplifying it. Finally, it practices the nuance of tone so that what's said in a poem is not the whole creation.

❧ Lining Up Surrealism

The Exercise

Surrealism can be both an image and an action. Typically, it exhibits a recombination of things or actions in an interesting and non-literal way. Consider James Wright's line "Last night I devoured the wing / of a cloud" or his reference to "the shafts of house."

Write a number of surrealistic images and actions that combine elements in ways that are not logical. Mix everyday objects and natural materials with unusual items; watch how dream-like images often take ordinary scenes in radical directions by introducing improbable elements or incidents. Context could be the key. Generate as many of them as you can.

Then compose a poem around one or more of your images and actions; use medium-length lines for your draft.

The Purpose

This exercise almost forces poetry out of us. Sometimes concentrating on the unusual line allows for expressions that are fresh, while other times focusing on juxtaposing these images can release power. Surrealism seems to lend itself well to shorter or medium-length lines and is a primary technique and practice of some of the world's best poets.

❧ Spin-offs

The Exercise

If you've been constructing an anthology or copying lines of poems into your Writer's Notebook, use selections from those. If not, browse anthologies of contemporary poems for a sentence or a phrase from another writer that you find remarkable/unforgettable (it could be a poet, fiction writer, artist, essayist, physicist, etc.) and use it as the title of a poem. Spin off that original sentence or a phrase to go deeper into something the passage doesn't explore, or let the phrase take you into a whole new place or feeling.

In your revised version, you could create a title of your own and use the originating line as an epigraph between the title and the body of the poem. Be sure to provide the writer's name and the title of your source, in any case.

Variation: Use a line from one of your own previous poems as the basis of your spin-off. You can think of your old line as the opening of the new one, the title, or the final line to which the poem must lead. If your project has sufficient energy, you might end up with a whole series of poems.

The Purpose

Artistic energy is transferable; this is especially true perhaps of the written or spoken word. In the same way that we read before we write in order to gather ideas or energy, here we actually pick up and use a beautiful thread acquired elsewhere and amplify it or change its direction. We move from simply manipulating others' words to using them as a springboard into the churning waters ourselves. It is an old and often used trick that poets use other writers in this way.

❧ Everybody Wants Something

The Exercise
Collect three to five personal ads, but strive for a variety in age, marriage and family status, gender, etc. Pay attention to how people describe themselves, as well as written and hopeful descriptions of the person from whom they wish to receive an answer. Notice that the one who placed the ad knows what he or she wants and can articulate that in their writing.

Write a poem from the point of view of a person (first person) who fits that description. The poem does not have to be about the matchmaking, the ad or the person who placed the ad (it can, of course, but it doesn't have to). After you get a draft, consider what that person really wants. Assume that he or she has a secret desire: it is unknown or she or he isn't ready to admit it yet. Revise your poem so that what that person wants slips out.

Variation I: The person writing the ad has *told* something about what he or she is like (shy or fun-loving or whatever). Imagine this person in a particular place—his or her apartment or vacation spot, at work, or in a place he or she wants to share with someone. Now write a poem that *shows* her or his qualities through action, imagery, or description located in that place.

Variation II: Write a poem about the moment of deciding to write the ad (or of deciding to actually send it in and pay for it) in the voice of that person.

Variation III: What do you want? Write a poem that shows who you are and the kind of person you'd like to be with (and why perhaps). Try not make it sound exactly like a personal ad; rather, try for a blend of ad language and poetry.

It is sometimes a danger to view those who place these ads as desperate or somehow "damaged goods," and the resulting poems can suffer from an ungenerous spirit, so we suggest adopting a sympathetic attitude toward your subject, even while perhaps identifying his or her foibles.

The Purpose
This exercise explores the subjective side of expressed public desires, an unusual action for most people. Because it also reinforces voice and personae while practicing the classic "showing vs. telling" principle of many creative writing classes, its benefits compound and collaborate.

❧ Chants
—adapted from Barbara Drake

The Exercise
Compose a whole series of sentences beginning with one or two of the following openings. Alternate between the literal and metaphorical; when you get to the end, open yourself up to the fantastic, surreal, or absurd.

I remember…	When…	The sky is…
I am afraid of…	The law of…	Through that door…
Who can say…	To think…	The earth is…
She was my…	I swear…	He was my…
From now on…	Do you…	I want…
Yesterday…Today…Tomorrow…		
I am the daughter (son) of…		

Compose a poem that uses long lines and repetition (see Walt Whitman's "To Think of Time" or others; or W.S. Merwin's "Psalm: Our Fathers"; various Navaho and other native songs). You don't have to begin each line with your phrase, but use it repeatedly so that it is integral to the overall poem.

The Purpose
This exercise shows how a repeated phrase can become a baseline or established rhythm for a poem and gives us practice in recognizing the line between meaningful repetition and monotony (which is usually discovered once crossed). The chant is a powerful, almost universal way of using language, either in writing, in speech or in song.

❧ The American Ghazal
(* First employed in Middle Eastern literature, the ghazal produced fascinating poems notable for their repeating themes and rhythmic return to an idea. Our version is a modest variation based loosely on the original, though the form of the ghazal was fairly flexible and open to begin with.)

The Exercise
This exercise, like the Villanelle that follows, also involves repetition but not of an entire line. Write a poem based on a central feature—a place, a person, an idea, a color—anything that strikes you. Begin the poem with a reference to your central feature. Next, use your central idea as a repetition at the end of the second line of each stanza in your poem. If your place feature were Cleveland, for example, you would repeat "in Cleveland" (or something similar) as the second line of each stanza. Aside from this pattern you are free to explore the writing and organization of your poem in any way you like.

The Purpose
Using a repeating theme develops in us a sense of rhythmic recursion or return that enhances our subject if done well. It also allows us to explore variations on our theme since we know that we

must return to it, yet at the same time the relative freedom of the form allows for a mostly liberated exploration of language otherwise. This exercise, like the one before it, also illustrates the difference between repetition that is somehow essential and musical and one that is mechanical and monotonous.

❧ The Free Verse Villanelle
(* The best known villanelles are Dylan Thomas' "Do Not Go Gentle into That Good Night," Elizabeth Bishop's "One Art," and Theodore Roethke's "The Waking.")

The Exercise
Free-write for a while about something comedic or serious that is on your mind. Read what you have written and look for a line that would be good if it were repeated a few times in a poem about your subject. Compose a poem in which you repeat this line as lines 1, 6, 12, and 18. You may end at line 18 or write one more line.

Variation: Read a variety of sample villanelles, search the internet for fuller discussions of the requirements and write one of your own.

The Purpose
This exercise provides an opportunity to explore the musical and rhythmic potential of preset repetition. Although the planned nature of the repetition may appear formulaic at first, the rhythmic chant established through it can produce a landslide effect, adding ideational depth and sparking new realizations or fresh ways of articulating—though these may not be achieved the first time through. This is a challenging form, so don't give up easily: keep trying!

❧ Blooming Personae

The Exercise
If you've done work on Mythology Forward, From the News, or The Poem You Can't Forget, you might return to them as a place to start. If not, try to come up with a dramatic, historic or comedic moment that it would be fun and fruitful to explore from a number of different people's points of view. Consider a myth or Biblical story, a news event, or a family incident. The key is that it should be one event with a variety of people involved.

Write a poem with several sections, or a series of poems, each exploring individual perspectives on the moment. Each should be in the first person. You can retell parts of the story, of course, but some people's emphases may be on the back story or the ramifications of that moment.

The Purpose
This exercise provides us with practice in developing different speakers or personae and using them to explore a scene or a situation. It emphasizes the variety of perspectives rather than the drama of story. These "domino" exercises require some perseverance, but they are worth it.

41

🍂 The Everyday Object Poem

The Exercise
Look around your house, yard, or apartment for everyday objects. Make a list of things that are often overlooked. Also, consider objects with personal significance to you or to someone you know.

Write a poem or a series of poems about or from the point of view of these objects. You may personify the doorstop for example or choose to write from the point of view of the lovers of compass, spoon, or wheelbarrow (it sounds crazy but let's see what happens). Let your imagination explore the possibilities; they are nearly endless.

The Purpose
The lives of everyday objects are a way of questioning and expanding our intimacy with things around us while at the same time interpreting the world through our deep humanity. What we end up saying about these objects is often a clear reflection of how we are feeling or thinking of our own lives and those of people we know and love. Sometimes, however, this exercise also allows us to tap into that strange energy that comes from pure imagination, a speculation without realistic roots. There are opportunities for humor or mock heroics in this exercise, as well. See almost any of Pablo Neruda's *Elemental Odes*.

🍂 Bestiary
(* Poets as different as Anne Sexton, Pablo Neruda, and Kenneth Rexroth have all found this kind of series exciting to write, even though the form goes back to the Middle Ages This simple structure has been used to teach the alphabet, to impart morals, to entertain children, and many more, and so it provides a framework that poets can use for a number of purposes.)

The Exercise
Make a list of animals you like, are curious about, are afraid of. From that list choose a few and look them up in an encyclopedia searching for trivia that is intriguing to you. "The dragonfly has a life span of twenty-four hours," or "A tiger's skin is also striped like their fur" are good examples of what you may find. Or you might try to answer the question, "Why is it called a 'dragon' fly?"

Now write a series of poems—each about a different animal—that somehow uses your tidbits. These can be about your animal or some idea (such as how brief any life is) or both. Try to generate five to ten poems from this exercise.

The Purpose
Tapping into the mythological view of animals has a number of advantages, including the fact that animals on their own have a considerable attraction for many readers. "Bestiary" also helps us generate and internalize a structure for a series that both possesses depth and can be departed

from and returned to in many ways. Using this exercise, poets often find themes that they can approach from different directions, either deliberately or by inclination and predisposition.

❧ Imitating a Translation

The Exercise
Find a collection of poems in translation (*The Vintage Book of World Poetry* is a good one but any will do). Read through it making note of the particular syntax, tones and strategies of the poems there. Try to deliberately write a poem that sounds like one or more you've been reading. Don't be afraid to borrow words, concepts or phrasings.

Variation: If you are reasonably skilled in a language other than English, try writing a poem in that language. (You may want to read some poems in the language first to familiarize yourself with its particular poetic syntax/diction.) Next, translate it into English. When you are finished, ask yourself, "How well does this work as a poem in English? Why or why not?"

The Purpose
This exercise explores the sometimes unusual tone, syntax and structure that often characterize poetry in translation. Of course, this is tricky because that syntax, language, and imagery arise out of a particular culture and may not translate very well or easily into ours. Exploring poetry from other cultures, however, is always a good idea, and borrowing techniques can also renew our own language and sensibilities, even revolutionize them.

❧ Past Life Monologues
—adapted from exercise by Joy Nolan
(* Although we are each aware that we have been different in the past, we don't necessarily imagine ourselves as having different "roles" or identities back there. But this is precisely what we are interested in exploring through this exercise.)

The Exercise
Consider your various phases in life and the many things you've done. Make a list of the kinds of people you've been. Give each a title. For example, if you got caught taking some candy from Sullivan's when you were in early elementary school, you could call yourself The Shoplifter or The Kleptomaniac. Search your past for general trends and isolated incidents and try to generate ten to fifteen of these "past lives."

Choose one of these, and imagine that person as a grown-up. Whatever trait the title captures is an important part of his or her character. Write a poem in the first person from the point of view of that "character." It does not have to deal with the events of the past but can be written from daily life now.

Variation I: Write a dramatic monologue in which this character addresses the self you grew up to become. Or compose a monologue addressing this person you could have been.

Variation II: Try writing the poem using your identity as a metaphor. In other words, if you are not a literal thief, what do you steal now? Time? Love? Freedom?

The Purpose
Past Life Monologues transforms the details and events of our lives into content for our poems and affords us the opportunity to consider or reconsider identity as a flexible thing capable of assuming different forms at different times. The particular energy associated with identity—which changes over the course of a lifetime—is used to fill the body of this work.

❧ Extended Cento

The Exercise
Return to the passages and quotations from others gathered in your Writer's Notebook; or if you haven't done this, begin gathering another writer's words—someone you find important, moving or interesting in some other way—as a recurring part of a poem of your own.

These "inserts" should help stimulate your thinking and writing and contribute to the development of your poem. The trick here is to not rely too heavily on the writing that is not your own but to proceed sparingly. You may include your inserts as separate sections to a poem, for example, or simply integrate them into the verse in a more natural way. We've seen this exercise done with personal letters, obituaries, philosophical writings, famous poems, and so on. You choose, but spend some time reflecting on what kind of text would be fruitful in producing a poem.

For examples, see Robert Hayden's "Middle Passage," about the slave trade and the ship Amistad.

The Purpose
When done well, this exercise creates an intentional, albeit a one-sided collaboration that can be very rewarding. Like many of our exercises, one of Extended Cento's purposes is to use others' words as an inspiration, a spotlight and a springboard, but it also refines the skill of manipulating tone shifts caused by vocabulary, perspective, and other differences in texts.

❧ Squinting at the Sun
(* Return perhaps to the Memory Storehouse and work you did on The Poem You Can't Forget; identify events that are too powerful to look at directly. See if you can come at these subjects indirectly. These can include emotional traumas, memories that are less than clear but still intriguing, complicated relationships, and so on.)

The Exercise
Begin writing, if you can, the event itself—a description of the persons involved or the place—but when it gets "too bright" turn aside and write about something else nearby, physically or

emotionally. Allow this rhythm to continue back and forth until you feel you've seen the whole of it. Revision will be more delicate, but this can result in a strong beginning.

The Purpose

This exercise seeks to reach, discover, and explore subjects that are sometimes difficult to write about and to learn how to use metaphors to contain feelings without having to name the particulars of the subject directly. This technique is very useful with difficult material and may be a more secure way to deal with issues involving family or others who might be embarrassed by the subject(s).

❧ The Illustrated Manuscript

—adapted from M.C. Richards

(* For this exercise the teacher or group leader will need a flip chart, or some other large piece of paper for each participant, some instrumental music of varying tempos and moods, plus markers, crayons, paints, or other drawing materials. If done alone, play the music for a while but shift it so that its feeling leads or redirects you at times. Another way to do this is to select music that moves you, leave it on, and allow yourself to be absorbed in the painting part.)

The Exercise

Using a sheet of flip chart or other large paper, draw, scribble, paint, or graffiti one side of it. If necessary, allow the work to dry thoroughly. While it is drying, write about the process, thoughts that came to mind, feelings that passed through you.

Fold the sheet in half, then half again, and the same once more until it is just about square. Leave one side folded, like a book binding, but slice open the others so the pages can turn. Some will be blank and some will be illustrated.

Now take one painting-page at a time, look at it, and allow it to suggest to you shapes and stories, images and impressions. Compose a poem for the facing page.

We usually write the poem on a separate piece of paper to allow for revisions, but we've seen it done immediately and spontaneously. We've also constructed a cover and page of contents once all the pages are full.

Variation: Consider a person with whom you need to be in greater communion—it could be someone who has already died, a part of yourself, a person from the past you have no contact with. (We've done this with a friend to whom we wanted to write a letter; we sent her the book as well.) Then go through the above process with that person in mind.

The Purpose

With this exercise, we want to access parts of the creative mind that language may obscure, to enjoy a rest from words, and to experience the correspondences between making visual images and verbal ones. Whenever we've done this exercise with groups, the privacy and wordlessness is a welcome respite, often opening writers to new vistas in their writing. It also has the by-product of deepening a class or writing group atmosphere.

❧ The Free Verse Sonnet

(* The free verse sonnet is a poem in 14—Shakespearean—or 16—Spenserian—lines. Unlike Shakespeare's or Spenser's versions, however, the poem does not have to rhyme or even contain a particular metrical pattern. Forcing our poems into a fixed number of lines changes the way we make decisions during the writing process and forces closure or development, depending upon our writing styles and the typical length of one of our poems.)

The Exercise

Write a series of poems 14 (or 16) lines in length on any subject you like: love, work, death, farm life, the city, prison, the inner city, the suburbs, bus stations, airports, etc. Try to explore a number of different aspects of your subject and paint a complete picture of it in all of its features—good and bad.

Variation: Read contemporary examples of these sturdy forms (*The Oxford Book of Sonnets* and *Strong Measures: Contemporary American Poetry in Traditional Forms* have plenty). Research the fine points of sonnet structure, and try your own strict version.

The Purpose

Formal poetry is often resisted by beginning writers because it may appear to prevent expression of what we really want to say, but as we get familiar with any form, we sense the ways it encourages new expressions. The trick here is to force ourselves to make different decisions from the ones we usually feel free to make in constructing a poem. This practice has the capacity to also force new thinking out of us and therein lies the virtue. It can also show us ways that form intensifies expression: that constraints in some directions force innovation in others.

❧ The Sensuous Orange

The Exercise

In silence, giving one piece of fruit your whole attention (we find oranges most effective) and all five of your senses, peel and eat an orange. Give yourself a fixed period—say 20 minutes. Afterward, free-write about the experience for another fifteen to twenty minutes.

Integrate your sensory details into a poem. Some use the experience itself, some write about the orange, some utilize the experience more metaphorically (for a love scene), and some explore tone (scientific/dissection versus erotic/undressing). Try several approaches.

Later, try this kind of sensuous attention with other things—your hair, a friend, sneakers, a car. If the thing has significance for you, you can begin to add specific memories associated with it as well.

The Purpose

Like the subjects of your Everyday Object Poems, food connects us to the world in ways we mostly ignore, so this exercise not only practices sensual awareness and choosing sensory detail, it helps us to attend to the life of the senses and to develop language that is based in those details.

It can lead to themes that the immediate subject would not have suggested initially. See the work of Diane Ackerman for an example of how this is done well.

❧ The New Shaped Poem
—after the designs of Douglas Holleley

(* For our version of the shaped poem, we provide a twist. *Don't* shape your poem into something representing your content in a literal way: wings for a poem about birds, a tree shape for a poem about nature, etc. Those are called concrete poems. Our version takes us into other possibilities.)

The Exercise

Take a poem whose "shape" has stalled (or any other poem that you are interested in trying this with) and imagine how manipulations of its overall shape on the "canvas" or photography paper of the page might enhance its visual qualities. Thinking of the page as a field and the poem as what lives in it might enliven your poem.

You might try bending the left margin so it looks like it is a being blown by a hidden wind or generate a swaying motion with a margin that swoops in and out. In another option, you can imagine your words getting farther and farther apart as they move down the page in what are otherwise fairly regular lines, as if the poem itself were coming apart as it goes along. If you have a friend who is a visual artist, consult with him or her about your project; get feedback and/or collaborate.

The Purpose

Emphasizing the visual aspects of a poem in this way frees us from the rigidity of the margins and the typical ways of using them. This technique can also jar the imagination, resulting in new rhythms or phrasing, new ways of arranging our images, or new voicings. Finally, in this exercise the visual status of the poem is taken to a new level. Some more traditional readers may find the results unusual or even distracting, but visual artists and experimentalists will be intrigued. New techniques always come with some risk, but they are also one way art evolves.

Chapter Five

Revision

For the last section of this book, we observe that finishing a draft usually brings a rush of satisfaction. In grand terms, we have just created something that did not exist before. Many writers talk about their most recent work with excitement and affection because of this; however, with time, they turn more critically to that work. Why?

To writers who haven't experienced its insights and rewards, revision can be drudgery. Even worse, some think if they change a poem, they will ruin it or lose the original feeling. We invite you to be fearless here because unlike painters, poets always retain their earlier drafts, so nothing is ever lost. More importantly, we hope you have the mysterious experience inherent in the process of returning to drafts because it can involve the same sort of inspiration as writing initially, though not in the same way. To unravel the revision mystery a little, consider a few of the many metaphors for revising, as well as the implications of those figures.

• "Fine-tuning": the piece of writing is like an engine. This way of thinking assumes all the parts are in place; the engine actually turns over and runs but only chugs along.

• "Polishing": as if the piece is a gem. This assumes the stone has been mined and removed from its surrounding material. Further, it's been cut into a pleasing shape; this view might even assume the gem shone once and is just a little smudged.

• "Brushing up": as if the poem might be a shoe, coat of suede, or a set table with cloth. The first two assume that the material has texture or nap, but it needs to stand up more. The second assumes the cloth and silverware are clean and set, the dishes are selected and arranged, and the meal is on its way, except a few crumbs need to be removed.

You get the idea. Behind revision there are other choices. Beginning writers of all kinds, not just poets, think of revision as a matter of wording (of "getting it right"), while more seasoned writers see it as a process that clarifies the concept and the way to best arrange that idea. For these writers, revision is not just removing or changing words. It involves developing (adding or deleting material), arranging (ordering and placing things), and structuring (opening, closing, considering the movement of ideas, and more).

A friend of ours once put it like this: "When looking at a poem-in-progress, don't admire what it is. Ask yourself what it could be."

The exciting thing for seasoned writers is also what may be maddening for beginning writers: the possibilities are endless. Someone once said that a piece of writing is never finished; it is merely abandoned. So we must find a happy balance between dashing things off (being satisfied too early) and obsessing to the point of never letting a poem rest and perhaps even making it worse over time.

These exercises are designed to explore the methods and goals of revision with the hope that you have a felt-experience of what that process can offer you. If you learn the principle of overall conception of your poems, their structure and ordering; of discovering the central concern in one of your elusive drafts; or of the ways language itself can inspire you, then these exercises have served their purpose—regardless of what's happened to this or that individual poem!

❧ Recognizing Warm Up & Explanation

(* Sometimes a draft of a poem announces the topic, describes the poet writing the poem, or otherwise rummages around before finding its subject. As necessary as these may feel or however integral they may seem to the poem they introduce, they might be slowing the reader down from the most rewarding parts. The old saying, "Start strong, end strong" holds here, too.)

The Exercise

Look at your drafts and imagine each poem beginning later, say after the first sentence or stanza. Draw a line on your draft indicating a new possible starting point. Furthermore, imagine cutting the material above that line or moving it, all or part, to another section of the poem. Of course, it changes the piece, but what is gained in doing so?

Now, analyze the endings of stanzas in the poem for lines that explain an image, the poem, or a final idea. This time, draw a line after these parts, and look to see if the earlier material is sufficient without that which follows. Look again at all material being explained in the poem and re-imagine it as imagery that, on its own, might resonate beyond explanations. You may need to move and/or recast existing lines to set up such imagery.

The Purpose

This exercise focuses our attention on the first material of a poem and facilitates an evaluation of it. Some poets find their initial work dispensable, as warm-up writing that is essential to the *process* of creating the poem, but in the finished draft is not needed; other poets realize that those opening lines are the heart of the poem but are lost without critical set-up material. This exercise also loosens up the structure of a draft and makes it possible to imagine other versions of the same material through a re-ordering of the elements for wholly different effects.

❧ Finding the Fire

(* Beware: this exercise beats this metaphor nearly to death, but "nearly" is key.)

The Exercise

You are trying to identify the draft's central concern or motivation, so read your drafts feeling for the "hottest" spots: phrases of startling honesty or revelation, moments of calm and clarity, passages that roll out smoothly but forcefully. Don't be too impressed with your own cleverness or skill in phrasing; that can be just smoke. Look for signs of something greater.

When you find it, consider the overall structure of the piece. Is the fire surrounded by unnecessary material? Does the other material fuel the fire, leading into it and out of it effectively or would putting them in another order help? Try opening up space with stanzas. Does that show you a new order or any extraneous detail that would allow it to burn hotter?

Maybe the fire lacks combustible material. The story may need to be told more fully or the image may need crucial detail. Try writing more, more, more. See if other points of view or other voices are possible.

Finally, perhaps the wood is just too "green." Perhaps what you need to do is to write everything you can somewhere in private and save it for later. Maybe you can't handle this material, and so you have to play it safe for fear of losing control. Season the material for as long as it takes. You've already got some starts; you've lost nothing.

The Purpose
This exercise gives us practice in identifying what is at stake in a poem, what is necessary in it, then arranging the work to be in synch with that awareness.

❧ The Second Version

The Exercise
Take a draft you are struggling with and title it. Put it aside for a period, at least overnight. When you return to it, start fresh by putting the title on a blank page with this addition: "version 2." Now write a whole new poem about the same subject. Consider point of view, other images, new metaphors, entirely different ways of coming at it (sonnet? letter poem? maybe one of the other exercises would spark you?) Repeat this exercise, as many times as necessary, in order to get a draft that seems essential or definitive to you. You may blend several versions into a poem that is more comprehensive, like a found poem from your own materials.

Variation: Return to a poem you wrote a long time ago, one you would never write today. Take the title and write about the same subject disregarding the earlier version as above.

The Purpose
The Second Version helps us approach a subject from a different perspective. This means of revising is attractive to less experienced poets who see revision as problematic, so remember the purpose here isn't to make this one's sole means of revision but as a way of opening a subject to deeper possibilities. Sometimes the approach we use in an initial draft takes on a life of its own, and clinging to this version of the poem could keep you from a better one about the same thing. The subject may not be not exhausted.

❧ Ruin This Poem

The Exercise
Identify the abstract words or phrases in a draft, and translate each one into language that appeals to the senses. Create images for statements.

Likewise, identify all the concrete particulars in this same draft, and translate each into its abstract message.

Leave all these jottings alone for a period for time, at least overnight. When you return, evaluate the ideas and how they are expressed, selecting from your lists images where needed and statements where needed.

The Purpose
The creative writing saying "Show rather than tell" and William Carlos Williams's self-contradictory statement "No ideas but in things" encourage us to evaluate what images convey, but they don't free us from the necessity to state things also. This exercise shows us options in how things are expressed, as well as illustrates the redundant, mysterious, or commonplace.

❧ Finding the Seams

(* Here is a teaching or workshop tip: Sometimes this is easier if the poem is not yours to begin with. We sometimes model this exercise using an overhead projector either with a published poem or one of our own.)

The Exercise
Take a draft and identify the sections of it.

Draw a box around each image. Do they overlap? Does the poem look like a weird kind of robot?

Consider the feelings of the poem, both what you hoped to put there and what might be drawn from it that you had not intended.

Draw a box in a different color around the separate feelings, even if they are similar, only a different shade of mood or feeling. Again, do the boxes correspond? Are they spaced apart? Do they stack up? Is there only one large box?

Now that you can see the various sections of the poem, maybe the redundant or over-explained is clearer. Perhaps parts can be re-ordered for greater effect. Maybe there is just too much going on in the poem; the boxes reveal many shifts or separate ideas. Perhaps the seams need to be stitched tighter, or they could need to be loosened up to allow a little more breathing space.

The Purpose
This exercise helps us identify the sections or parts of a poem, then consider or reconsider their order. This detailed view of the poem is often illuminating. If most poems are composed of a number of parts, strategies or segments—whether we see them or not—then this exercise describes that phenomenon and uses it to our advantage.

❧ Rewiring the Speaker

The Exercise
Take a poem you have written in your own voice and draft a second version of it in the voice of a speaker who is not you, i.e. a "persona." Some writers change the "I" in the poem to "you" so that the speaker of the current draft is the one addressed in the new version, introducing another speaker into the dynamic. Others may wish to choose a persona who is related to the poem's original subject (another family member, for instance, if the poem is about familial relations).

Still others may choose a completely objective person, such as a judge, a neighbor, or a homeless person. Varying the distance of the speaker might bring the central concern of the poem into sharper relief than speaking it yourself.

Variation: Return to the exercise Blooming Personae and write several versions of the poem from the perspectives of different people. Compare the versions of the poems that you produce and critically assess their values, what each of them offers or takes away from the subject at hand.

The Purpose
By "rewiring" the speaker in our poems, we confront what we think the poem is about by testing another speaker's view of it. This challenges our concepts and our knowing at a basic level and can certainly confirm our writing as a path to self-discovery.

❧ Seven Ways from Somewhere

The Exercise
Take a draft that you think has settled into its language and images; you aren't considering the words or figures here. Re-break your lines and re-arrange your stanzas. Do this six times so that you have seven different versions of the same poem. Try long lines and short ones. Try line breaks that increase a sense of flow and ones that put rocks in the stream. Leave these revisions for a time, at least overnight. When you return to them, consider the gains and losses of your decisions on each line and integrate your versions into what is now the eighth poem.

The Purpose
This practice pushes us beyond habit and expectation in our lines to discover new ways of using them. It confronts us with our assumptions and asks us to reconsider the *effects* of line length, line breaks, stanza placement, and stanza structure.

❧ The Double Bloom
—adapted from J. D. McClatchy

The Exercise
Triple space your draft, perhaps even changing the font to one you don't really care for but can read easily.

Read each line separately and write a new line out of the one you've got. Don't try to set up the next printed line; just follow the suggestions, possibilities and new directions offered by each individual line, as you did in the Collaborative Poem.

Sometimes a line will bloom into several inside the original. Listen also for whole new images or rhythms that might be missing in the original poem. Some of the new material might be integrated into the poem, or it might become another version of the same one, or it might be revised into its own work.

The Purpose
"The Double Bloom" exercise explores occasions in the poem that are currently closed, and this enables us to experience suggestions existing lines make. It can also develop new material in poems that seem somehow incomplete.

❧ Stanza Regular, Stanza Interruptus

The Exercise
Take any of the poems you have generated in other exercises in this book and try stanza breaks that end with the sentence endings in the poem itself. Think of the stanzas like paragraphs, a unit to contain a single thought.

Next, in the same poem try stanza breaks that occur in the middle of sentences in the poem itself, so that there is a unit of rhythm across which the unit of thought moves.

Compare these two versions of the poem and think about, or discuss with friends, what effects the differences in presentation generate. Don't simply look at the issue of whether it "flows" or not; look for new ambiguities, ways the breaks encourage readers to attend to words or ideas within sentences, or rhythms you hadn't heard before.

Finally, decide which one seems to suit the poem best.

The Purpose
This exercise lends either "stops" or "movement and momentum" to a poem's form. It demonstrates the gains and losses with each, and may help us to find out which is the right choice for individual poems—or what blend of them is optimal. Discovering this often requires that we see such options and differences side-by-side in order to make the right call or decision.

❧ Fifty Ways to Leave Your Poem

The Exercise
Take any of the drafts you generated in other exercises in this book, and experiment with as many different forms as possible for that poem.

Try short lines with no stanzas: medium-length lines in two-, three-, four-, or five-line (ad infinitum) stanzas; alternating two- and four-line stanzas, and so on. Read it aloud listening for pauses, striving to score those hesitations in your arrangement on the page.

Try some elements of concrete poems, where the arrangement visually represents the content; try arrangements that only abstractly represent the content.

Remember that the page is only arbitrarily a rectangle stood on its end. Don't be afraid to "think outside the square" (or up-ended "rectangle" in this case) as you explore line and stanza lengths and breaks in considering a form for your poem.

The Purpose
Every poem requires the form that is right for it. Re-imagining line and stanza breaks can often energize a poem we may have lost interest in and show us something new in the words. Keeping the material consistent as we change the arrangement can isolate the effects of individual choices in ways that may not be obvious if those arrangements are attempted earlier in the life of a draft. This exercise can also dramatize the poem's central urgency in ways that help us recognize extraneous material as well.

❧ The Blooming Book
—adapted from David Citino, via Philip Terman
(* We end our exercises in revision in particular and this book as a whole with a suggestion about one way books of poetry, or chapters of them, are planned and written.)

The Exercise
Identify a single poem that has a particular resonance for you. Imagine this one piece growing into a series, maybe even a whole book of poems.

Do whatever you need to do to keep the group blooming: don't be afraid to do a little research— seek out pictures and art, make visits to locales, interview people; brainstorm a list of titles for potential poems; highlight lines in this draft you might try as "spin-offs"; consider this poem's central theme to see if it is one you could explore via personae; brainstorm everyday objects that touch on this theme.

Try to imagine how this poem might branch out into a series of poems exploring your subject(s) more fully. Over several months with a diligent work ethic, see if you can get the initial poem to bloom into a group of poems.

The Purpose
We include this exercise in our section on revision because it is a true "re-envisioning" of purpose for a single significant poem and therefore will appeal particularly to all serious practitioners of the art of revising. Good luck!

❧

Appendix
of
Selected Student Poems

Generated by *Exercises for Poets: Double Bloom*

❧ From "The 'Bad' Poem Exercise"

The Bad Poem

I love you

and you love me

I think our love

was meant to be

I think of you

And sometimes I cry

without your love

I would die

if you leave,

I'll be so sad

and that would be

not good, but bad

so I'll love you forever,

you'll see

that our love

was meant to be.

—*Christine Neer, Corning Community College*

From "Image Electricity"

Untitled

Stop. The wind cannot

Be captured in golden nets

Woven with silk, glossy threads.

Twist open the jar bursting

From your pocket. Run wild

At the gust and charge into

The breeze, open jar held high,

Tilted towards the flow. Encase

Your prize. Look and listen,

And discover.

Stop.

You cannot hold the wind

Inside an empty jar.

—Travis Morris, Ohio University—Lancaster

Lonesome

A lonely lamppost

Illuminating puddles of a storm.

It has a place,

A job to do,

But it is only loved in the night.

—A.J. Bernard, Ohio University—Lancaster

❧ From "The Prose Poem"

New Junction

New junction was small, and its only stoplight, controlling the perpendicular flow, from Main Street onto Long Hill, hung in the center of town. Most of its inhabitants lived on Main, but plenty of others in its host of thick backwoods and country pastures. A visitor coming in along main could choose right or left at the single light and cruise downhill into New Junction's night life or sputter uphill into multiple mansions and cleaner streets. However, visitors seldom came to New Junction, but when they did, whether it be a joyride or a break from big city stress, they always seemed to come browsing into town around sunset, just as New Junction was balanced between light and dark.

—Justin Carson, Ohio University—Lancaster

❧ From "Who Will You Become?"

Untitled

His grandfather's spirit rises

sometimes in a blue billow, sometimes—

with the deepest concentration, and

most artful of oral form

—in a perfect torus.

He lightly pounds the earth, careful

not to extinguish the flame, and reflects

upon the treacherous heirlooms

that will one day take his son.

—Nathan Riggs, Ohio University—Lancaster

❧ From "Writing a Portrait"

Mi Abuelita

Her fingers told
stories of misplaced memoirs,
fresh mangoes and yucca
They mused over days of
birthday dresses, hidden money,
the morning cigarette

Plastered on her palms–
scratches from concrete block,
scenes of violent affection,
retribution and a dishrag

Her wrists were tired–
bound by hostility,
four babies to feed,
bags from the market

Remembering the unity
her hands revealed

—Amber Howell, Ohio University—Lancaster

From "Small Research Nature Poem"

Snowfall

Cold, moist kisses against my cheeks.

Frozen dewdrops on my eyelashes.

Sweet, dewy dampness on the end of my tongue.

Dots of white, glittering in my hair like a halo.

The scent of a crisp, clean perfume,

Wafting through

The muffled night air.

A silent, crisp, glistening whiteness.

A damp, cool, icy joy.

Pieces of clouds swirl past me.

White winds; swirling,

falling stars.

—Amy Terry, Corning Community College

❧ From "The Poem You Can't Forget"

Chris

pale and hard, like raw clay

set perfectly into a smile

that never existed.

every hair in place, every

lash curled, the deep gash

no one had seen before, hands

that used to move constantly

now lying anxious for the next

step—lips too pink, mortician's

lipstick to cover the blue. sweet

voice moved on to

better things, yellow hawaiian

shirt and the flowers

just strong enough to make me gag.

please, oh please tell me it was

the flowers.

—*Rachel Miller, Ohio University—Lancaster*

❧ From "The Found Poem"

"Death Song"

Found poem from Dee Brown's
Bury My Heart at Wounded Knee

in a horseshoe bend

north of an almost dry streambed

the Cheyenne camp lay.

warriors hunting   miles away

six hundred Indians   women and children

in a horseshoe bend lay.

fire opened by soldiers

in gray light of winter down.

Nothing lived long.

an American flag   tied to a lodge pole

absolute safetyfluttering

lazily.

Mountains shot down

With arms folded.

only the earth halted momentarily.

—Michael Crane, Corning Community College

From "The Poem Buyout"

Field of Dreams

Along the playing field
spectators arriving daily
some old, some young.

Men, women and children,
first ones got the best seats
awfully gaudy though.

Must want to be seen,
others sit low, spaced apart.
More small seats than not,

Like the bleachers, I guess
although everyone wants the upper deck.
Not everyone makes it.
In no hurry for this game.

—*Joseph Moglia*

From "Short-line Railroad"

Love Note

Crumpled and confused
Letters falling into place,
She hunts for understanding
beneath the bed, in the sheets

She would settle for composure,
but she spent it all
on a new pair of shoes
Now she's left to make the bed alone

She won't look in the mirror
Reflection is sure to point at her
like a mother during a hangover,
piercing and smug

She wipes black streaks
from her face and hangs her head
next to her heart,
while picking up petals
off of the floor

—Amber Howell, Ohio University—Lancaster

❧ From "Conversation in a Long Line"

Talking with Dennis in the breakroom

Not quite the scene you'd imagine for two grassroots to be talkin' about theology.

Thick, threatening? cigarette smoke was drenching my shirt, tearin' up our lungs, secretly

killing us as we sat there eating and trying to save our souls.

Supernatural stuff, meaning not normal-sounding, not of nature,

but of light, the Holy Ghost makin' people talk in crazy tongues and changing their lives

somehow.

That's what we talked about:

pornography, modesty, family, our life stories, old cigarette ashes scattered on the table,

reading the bible and how interesting it is.

Are you allowed to call a sacred book "interesting"?

As if it's just something to think about, not something that should tremble your life.

—Jen Eisnaugle, Ohio University—Lancaster

From "Everybody Wants Something"

Flying to Panama

Don't bury me in congested,
death-drenched soil.
Blaze my bones
In that roaring army of heat

Don't let me hide
under shadows,
roots of trees
blocking my view
Let me ride the wind
like a magic carpet

I could never
soak in musty earth,
wet with leftover weather
day after day
Give me an end

No vaulted home with
satin wallpaper,
smell of stone flowers
Give me freedom,
proclaiming my immortality
ash by ash
across the land

Furthermore –
I hate worms.

> —*Amber Howell, Ohio University—Lancaster*

❧ From "The Everyday Object Poem"

The Guitar

Cracked edges

Finger smudges

Thin layer of grime lay atop

fading laminate finish

and sturdy craftsmanship.

The neck

Arid

Worn down frets

display a sense of being used to the fullest, saying

I am a guitar

that's what I do.

Turning knobs, bridge pins

by comparison

shine new.

A thin layer of dust

concentrates

in the crevices of these parts.

But what makes this guitar unique

a diamond

a pearl in my eyes

is the extra piece of string that dangles of the head stock.

This piece of string

this short, spring like metal piece

Gyrates

with each strum of the rhythm.

Giving this inanimate object a sense of life.

— *J. Whitford, Corning Community College*

From "Squinting at the Sun"

Two Rivers

Rivers of blood

Flow through your face

Spit splinters of glass

Adorn your expression

Oh, my God

You can't walk

I think I'm going to be sick.

*

That man in the chair

Out the window

Been watching him for hours

Not sure what he is waiting for

Would think he would just ask

Someone to help him over the curb

Lots of people to ask

*

Beeping noises. . .driving me crazy

You don't know I'm here

Never seen you so black and blue

Please talk to me

It's lonely here

*

Look at that
Such a stubborn man
Won't ask for help
Struggles with the chair
Trying to maneuver over the curb
All by himself
He almost fell out

                *

Your eyes are open
Can't get used to the one
Filled with blood
You recognize me
Don't say anything
It's okay. . .just sleep

                *

Can't believe it
He whittled himself
Over the curb
Down the sidewalk he goes
Can't really see him anymore
It's getting dark.

        —Julie Ulrich, Ohio University—Lancaster